CHINESE
LITERATURE
FOR THE 1980s

CHINESE LITERATURE
FOR THE 1980s
The Fourth Congress of Writers & Artists

edited with an introduction by
HOWARD GOLDBLATT

M. E. Sharpe Inc.

ARMONK, NEW YORK
LONDON

Library of Congress Cataloging in Publication Data

Main entry under title:

Chinese literature for the 1980s.

    Compilation of 14 articles on the Fourth Congress and 2 articles on the
Third Congress translated from various sources by different translators.
    1. Arts—China—Congresses. I. Goldblatt, Howard, 1939– .
II. Chung-kuo wen hsüeh i shu kung tso che tai piao ta hui (4th:1979:Peking,
China)

NX583.A1C4524	700′.951	82-744
ISBN 0-87332-208-8		AACR2

Printed in the United States of America

To the memory of Kai-yu Hsu

CONTENTS

PREFACE

    In compiling this collection, the editor has been privileged to work with a team of talented and cooperative translators, many of whom had to work under almost unreasonable deadlines. Although consistency in terminology has been achieved, no attempt has been made to render the translators' styles uniform, for they were dealing with widely divergent styles in the original.

    The source is given for each piece for ease of reference, but since the dates for many of the selections could not be determined with precise accuracy, none have been given (Xiao Jun indicated to the editor that the published version of his speech is probably a combined version of two speeches he delivered, one to the main congress and one to the Writers Association). All of the selections have been translated in their entirety (how complete and faithful the published versions are in the original is anyone's guess), with the exception of the 25,000-word speech by Zhou Yang, which has been trimmed by approximately one-fourth, and the talk by Chen Dengke, from which several repetitive passages have been deleted (excised portions have been indicated by ellipsis marks). The pinyin system of romanization has been used throughout, with the exception of one or two familiar place-names.

    Special thanks are due to Betty Ting, who, in addition to her excellent translations, tirelessly searched for and supplied many of the speeches included here, and Douglas Merwin of M. E. Sharpe, Inc., who enthusiastically supported the original idea and remained extremely helpful and patient throughout the duration of the project. Since the editor had the last word on all matters of selection, organization, format, and translation, any errors are his responsibility.

    This volume is dedicated to the memory of my teacher, colleague, and friend, Professor Kai-yu Hsu of San Francisco State University, who died tragically on January 4, 1982, as this book was going to press. It was he who first recognized the significance of making

these reports and speeches available in translation, and who introduced me to the publisher; more than that, Professor Hsu's abiding
interest in Chinese literature and Chinese writers has provided a
stimulus for virtually every contributor to the anthology. His contributions to the field and his humanity will not be forgotten.

H. G.
Los Angeles
January 1982

INTRODUCTION

HOWARD GOLDBLATT

I

While literary trends in most societies are analyzed, debated, and understood in retrospect, post-Liberation China's literary trends and directions are generally announced beforehand. This gives China watchers the opportunity not only to appraise China's literature and art on its intrinsic merits, but to see how close to or far from the prescribed norms it is, then to attempt to predict what the official reactions will be. Formal gatherings of Chinese writers and artists and their leaders, therefore, are significant events, not because that is where literary and artistic policy is determined (hardly anyone believes that), but because it is often where it is aired publicly and where it is discussed, supported, and ultimately approved by the rank and file. Mao Zedong's famous "Talks at the Yan'an Conference on Literature and Art" (1942), where the Chairman laid down his guidelines for creative activity, set the precedent and the tone, and although his "Talks" are still held up as the fount of all socialist literary knowledge, they are currently being reevaluated by a leadership intent upon making interpretation rather than basic wisdom the issue at hand.[1]

On July 2, 1949, three months before Liberation, the First Congress of Chinese Writers and Artists was convened in Peking. At this gathering the All-China Federation of Chinese Literary and Art Circles was created, as were several affiliate organizations, including the Chinese Writers Association. The Second Congress was convened in September 1953, at which time the Chinese Writers Association and other affiliate organizations held their first national meetings; the Third Congress took place in July 1960. In February 1966, Jiang Qing convened the Forum on Literary and Art Work in the Armed Forces, in Shanghai, which ushered in the

Great Proletarian Cultural Revolution.

The Fourth Congress, the first following the Cultural Revolution and the first post-Mao congress (he died in 1976), was called for at the third plenary session of the All-China Federation of Chinese Literary and Art Circles from May to June 1978. The congress opened on October 30, 1979, in Peking and closed on November 16. In attendance were more than 3,200 writers and artists who belonged to the nine affiliate organizations.[2]

The opening address at the congress was made by the octogenarian vice-chairman of the Federation and chairman of the Chinese Writers Association, Mao Dun, on October 30. His comments were followed by Vice-Premier Deng Xiaoping's Congratulatory Message. The first major substantive address was given by the Federation vice-chairman, Zhou Yang, on November 1. Lasting more than four hours, his report comprised a historical overview of modern Chinese literary and artistic developments and achievements since the founding of the nation, a close look at the current literary scene, and the announcement of Party policy and goals. The emotional highlight of the congress came on that same day when the playwright Yang Hansheng read a speech entitled "An Expression of Mourning for Writers and Artists Hounded to Their Deaths and Wrongly Vilified by Lin Biao and the Gang of Four," during which he gravely intoned the names of over a hundred deceased writers and artists.[3]

The Federation's affiliate organizations opened their week-long series of meetings and discussions on November 4, concerning themselves primarily with heated debates on the reports by Deng Xiaoping, Zhou Yang, and Mao Dun (whose second speech, "Emancipate Thought and Encourage Literary and Artistic Democracy," was also made to the entire assembly), the reading of prepared speeches by their members, and housekeeping duties such as charter revisions and the election of officers.

Following the closing ceremony on November 16, presided over by the octogenarian playwright Xia Yan, then-Party Chairman Hua Guofeng and then-Vice-Premier Hu Yaobang addressed the delegates.

II

Of the dozens of speeches and reports, all but a few were subsequently published in China or Hong Kong.[4] Sixteen have been translated for the present anthology: In addition to the opening and closing addresses to the congress and to the Chinese Writers Association, and Deng Xiaoping's Congratulatory Message, the selection process has been guided by the principle of broad representation. Speeches by older, middle-aged, and younger writers have been included, as have at least one speech each by a novelist, a dramatist, and a poet. Several pieces by writers who have been in trouble with the Party prior to or subsequent to the congress have also been selected. The styles of the speeches vary, from the slogan-laden pronouncements of literary and political leaders to the reminiscences of writers like Xiao Jun; from the formal writing style of the likes of Liu Baiyu to the evocative elegance of Ke Yan; and from the highly optimistic views of Ba Jin to the almost alarmist views of Chen Dengke.

Understandably, a number of themes are repeated in virtually every speech: support of China's Four Modernizations, strong anti-Gang of Four sentiments and indictments, general optimism regarding the future (running from cautious to absolute), a call for more intellectual freedom, renewed commitment to socialist ideals, and agreement on the important role of writers and artists in the furtherance of these ideals.

III

One of the most intriguing aspects of the speeches and reports from the Fourth Congress is how much the atmosphere has changed in the intervening two years. The liberalization process and the relaxation of Party controls have periodically given way to renewed strictures and a tightening of controls; the call for trailblazers (chuangjiang) has lessened with each appeal for noninterference by new writers and artists; some of the most outspoken "liberal" writers, such as Bai Hua, Liu Binyan, Wang Ruowang (not represented here), and Chen Dengke, have been subjected to the very criticisms they warned so eloquently and passionately against; and literary experimentation and innovation, for which the leadership called, have all too often been stifled. That is not to say that the literary scene has reverted back to a Cultural Revolution sterility, but that with the dissipation of the euphoria in evidence at the congress, where the carrot was so magnanimously proffered, the stick has made a frequent and occasionally alarming reappearance. Certainly, nothing approaching the horrors of the 1956 anti-rightist campaign or the Cultural Revolution has recurred, or seems likely to recur in the immediate future, and literary achievements have made steady, if belabored, progress. Still, there are signs that all is not yet well in China's literary and artistic circles. Evidence of this is not difficult to find:

The first major evaluation of the Fourth Congress came during a forum on dramatic arts held in Peking from January 23 to February 13, 1980.[5] Presided over by He Jingzhi and attended by Zhou Yang, Xia Yan, Cao Yu, and others, the forum featured a six-hour talk by the newly elevated general secretary of the Central Committee of the CCP, Hu Yaobang. Hu introduced a new controversy over some recent plays, although the general tone of the speech was conciliatory, the message one of accommodation and optimism. Hu candidly demythologized Mao by pointing out errors in his views of literature.

While making a number of concrete proposals regarding themes, the production of more and better literary works, how to swell the ranks of writers, and writers' responsibilities, Hu seemed most intent on reassuring members of the intellectual community that debate was to be encouraged, that society was better served by honesty and integrity than by rigid dogma, slogans, and the mechanical application of current political orthodoxies in literary works. He repeatedly guaranteed a more humanitarian position by the Party toward writers and artists and gave official sanction for them to continue with exposé literature, as long as its goal continued to be constructive and supportive of the modernization campaign. To this end, he promised a policy of noninterference in literary matters by the government and the Party.

Slightly more than a year and a half later (September 1981), following Hu's ascension to Party chairman, he did an about-face. In addressing the centennial anniversary of the birth of Lu Xun (Lu Hsün), Hu complained that China's writers had abused the freedoms they had been given at the Fourth Congress and that their rebelliousness would no longer be tolerated by the Party.[6] Unmindful of international public opinion, the Party was adopting a get-tough policy in handling all writers and artists who had lost sight of the socialist creed that everything is subordinate to politics and who were flirting with the heretical stance of "art for art's sake." Whether Hu's stern attack on intellectual freedom is just another swing of the pendulum or a permanent negation of the liberal posture assumed by the Party leadership in late 1979 is a question of lasting significance.

IV

Vice-Premier Deng's Congratulatory Message to the Fourth Con-

gress is an upbeat speech in which he sets the official tone. He
calls upon the nation's writers and artists to accentuate the positive—to scale down the anti-Gang of Four attack and work for
China's modernization drive—to learn from Western writers and
artists, and to guard against excesses from both the right and the
left. While upholding the inviolability of Chairman Mao's views on
literature, he denounces the narrow interpretation of literature and
art as mere tools of class struggle. In speaking to the leadership
and to literary critics, he demands an end to interference in the
choice of "subject matter and method of presentation based upon
artistic practice and exploration."

Zhou Yang, who has been the featured speaker at all four congresses, assumes in his speech a radically different tone from the
previous congress, where he attacked in a vicious and distorted
fashion such "counterrevolutionaries" as Ding Ling, Chen Qixia,
Feng Xuefeng, and others. In his latest speech he apologizes for
his earlier posture and even circulated the text of his speech for
comments and criticism before delivering it. For this he was
reportedly hailed as a man of courage and integrity by members of
the audience, although his speech was not universally acclaimed,
as Xiao Jun's comments make abundantly clear.

Zhou Yang echoes most of Deng Xiaoping's hopes and demands,
but is not only more precise and comprehensive in both his analysis
of China's literary and artistic achievements since Liberation and
his vision of the future, but is even more inclined to hold out the
olive branch. He speaks in unequivocal terms of the need for noninterference by bureaucrats and of the evils of personal deification
(specifically, the cult of Mao)—the latter an issue on which the
writer Bai Hua would speak even more forcefully. Zhou Yang con-
tends that the prime literary relationship is not literature and politics, but literature and the lives of the people. So that the people
will be better served, he demands that dogmatism and uniformity
be rejected and that the "needs of a given historical period" (itself
a two-edged sword) be well served by literary and artistic works
that expose societal ills as well as by those that praise socialism
and the Party. Nonetheless, the proof of the pudding is in the eating,
and one can assume that Zhou himself has participated in official
decisions that have subsequently nullified many of his own words.

Among those writers who might be characterized as belonging
to the "loyal opposition"—that is, those who were labeled "rightists"
during the 1950s and who are the most outspoken advocates of what

Mao Dun called "literary and artistic democracy" (wenyi minzhu)—
the most impassioned pleas are made by the writers Bai Hua, Liu
Binyan, and Chen Dengke. Bai Hua, who came under attack in 1981
by the People's Liberation Army Daily over a movie script he had
written (resulting in a nationwide mini-campaign), is almost pro-
phetic in his fears of what might happen if the leadership does not
stand by its promises, although he could not have guessed that it
would happen to him.

Liu Binyan, who has gained international recognition for his reportage, is the most analytical among the speakers presented here
and the one most given to anecdotal writing. Steering clear of slogans that grow increasingly meaningless with use, he attacks contemporary bureaucratic trends, analyzes the roots of leftism, and
warns against the tendency to conform to convention ("...in the
end even the language is monotonous, and all opinions...can be
expressed in some interchangeable formula").

Chen Dengke's speech reads like a modern-day "j'accuse." In
forceful, frank, and emotional language, he deals almost exclusively
with contemporary events and trends, leaving the wholesale vilifi-
cation of the Gang of Four to others (like Wang Meng). Fearing a
resurgence of campaigns against writers (one of which subsequently
involved him), he condemns those who are willing to lead or join
attacks against fellow writers for their own advancement. He then
takes the lead in making concrete recommendations to improve the
lives of writers and artists and to ensure their integrity.

Wang Meng, on the other hand, generally speaks in platitudes,
condemning Lin Biao and the Gang of Four for nearly all of society's ills and praising the Party in the most effusive terms imaginable. His sentiments are echoed by the youngest writer represented
here, Liu Xinwu, whose "The Class Counsellor" ushered in the post-
Gang of Four literary genre known as "literature of the wounded."

Among the most appealing selections are the speeches by Ke Yan
and Xiao Jun, the former for its poetic qualities and emotional appeal, the latter for its highly personal nature and almost cavalier
tone. Ke Yan, one of the editors of the poetry journal Shikan, con-
trasts literary achievements of the Cultural Revolution and the
three subsequent years by citing poems from both periods, injecting
some very personal and moving anecdotes to heighten the impact of
her talk.

Xiao Jun, the controversial Northeastern novelist, pulls no

punches in his diatribes against the various forces that removed him from the scene for thirty years, as well as the bureaucratic mentality that simply will not die.

Xia Yan, who appears twice in this anthology (as do Mao Dun and Liu Binyan, although Liu's second talk is intended to supplement the first), gives his listeners an overview of dramatic activities, past and present, then makes the standard appeals for better and more responsive plays and librettos.

In his closing address to the Chinese Writers Association, Ba Jin hedges on the issue of a future Gang of Four, but if there is one single thread running throughout this collection of speeches and reports, it is that such a holocaust must never happen again, that not only would literature and art suffer untold damage, but that China's economic and social structure could come crashing down once and for all. More than two years have passed since the Fourth Congress was convened, and no new Gang of Four has appeared. We can only hope that the literary and artistic communities continue their vigil to see that it doesn't happen and that the nation's leadership heed their words.

NOTES

1. For the text of Mao's "Talks" and analysis of it, see Bonnie S. McDougall, Mao Zedong's "Talks at the Yan'an Conference on Literature and Art": A Translation of the 1943 Text with Commentary (Ann Arbor: Center for Chinese Studies, The University of Michigan, 1980) and Merle Goldman, Literary Dissent in Communist China (Cambridge, Mass.: Harvard University Press, 1967).

2. They are: The Chinese Writers Association, Chinese Dramatists Association, Chinese Musicians Association, Chinese Artists Association, Chinese Film Workers Association, Chinese Dancers Association, Chinese Balladeers Association, Chinese Folk Literature and Art Association, and Chinese Photographers Association. The Chinese Acrobats Association was admitted at the Fourth Congress.

3. Including such creative writers as Lao She, Tian Han, Ah Ying, Zhao Shuli, Liu Qing, Zhou Libo, He Qifang, Zheng Boqi, Yang Shuo, Guo Xiaochuan, Li Guangtian, Meng Qiao, Sima Wensun, Huang Guliu, Fang Zhi, Xiao Yemu, Mu Mutian, and Shen Yinmo; literary critics and theoreticians Feng Xuefeng, Shao Quanlin, Wang Renshu, Liu Zhiming, He Jiahuai, Ye Yiqun, and Xu Maoyong; the translator Fu Lei; the musician Ma Ke; and the artist Feng Zikai.

4. Two anthologies were published in China in 1980: Zhongguo wenxue yishujie lianhehui, ed., Zhongguo wenxue yishu gongzuozhe disici daibiao dahui wenji (Chengdu: Sichuan renmin chubanshe, 1980) and Zhongguo wenxue yishu-

jie lianhehui, ed., Kaipi shehuizhuyi wenyi fanrong de xin shiqi (Chengdu: Sichuan renmin chubanshe, 1980).

5. Published in Guangjiaojing (Hong Kong), May 1980, pp. 27-40.

6. See Michael Parks, "Chinese Party Leader Scolds Writers, Artists for 'Negative Works,'" Los Angeles Times, September 26, 1981, p. I-9.

CHINESE LITERATURE
FOR THE 1980s

OPENING ADDRESS TO THE FOURTH CONGRESS OF CHINESE WRITERS AND ARTISTS

Mao Dun

Delegates and Guests:

The Fourth Congress of Chinese Writers and Artists is now in session.

The First Congress of Chinese Writers and Artists, held thirty years ago, was a great gathering of our country's writers and artists on the eve of the national victory that the Chinese people, under the leadership of the Party, attained by overturning the Three Big Mountains.* Our present meeting is another grand gathering of writers and artists following the momentous victory the Party and people achieved by smashing Lin Biao and the Gang of Four. Among the 3,200 delegates attending this congress are veterans of the literary world who have braved many storms and made outstanding achievements, new talents from the art and literary worlds who have just begun to display their ability and are full of youthful vigor, writers and artists from among our national minorities, and progressive, patriotic individuals from literary and art circles in Taiwan, Hong Kong, and Macao, representing the vast numbers of writers and artists of the nation. As all our countrymen raise the call to march courageously toward the Four Modernizations during these days of joyous celebration over the thirtieth anniversary of the founding of our nation, we happily assemble in this hall to discuss jointly the major issues on the literature and art fronts. This is a distinguished gathering of the literary and art worlds which holds great historical significance for China.

Today, Vice-Chairmen Ye Jianying, Deng Xiaoping, and Li Xiannian, as well as other Party and state leaders, are attending our opening ceremony. Participants in the congress also include dele-

---

*Imperialism, feudalism, and capitalism. — H. G.

gates of the National Federation of Trade Unions, the National Women's Federation, the Communist Youth League, and the People's Liberation Army, and comrades in charge of education, news, culture, and other related fields. Our eminent foreign friends, the Japanese critic Miyagawa Torao, the Dutch filmmaker Joris Ivens, and the British writer Felix Greene, honor our meeting with their presence. On behalf of this congress, I would like to pay tribute to the Party and the state leaders in attendance and extend a warm welcome to all the guests.

Comrades, nineteen years have already passed since the Third Congress of Writers and Artists in 1960. During this period, Lin Biao and the Gang of Four engaged in conspiratorial activities to seize supreme leadership of the Party and usurp state power. Literary and art circles were the first to be affected. The people's cause in literature and art was severely damaged and impaired. However, we can be proud that the overwhelming majority of writers and artists withstood the pressure of the counterrevolutionaries and, adopting various methods, waged a resolute and courageous struggle against them. The whip and cangue, insult and persecution, did not shatter us, but trained us to be even stronger and more mature. As the facts demonstrate, our ranks are strong and fearless, loyal to the Party, the people, and the socialist cause. We assemble here today to announce that the ultra-leftist line and subversive literature and art, promoted by Lin Biao and the Gang of Four, have ceased forever and that a new page has been turned in the history of socialist literature and art.

After smashing the Gang of Four, under the leadership of the Party and through the concern and support of the people and the concerted efforts of countless writers and artists, old and new, we broke the shackles of the spirit, criticized the ultra-leftist line, and redressed numerous unjust, false, and incorrect cases. During this struggle to restore order and emancipate thought, the garden of socialist literature and art became resplendent with color; the spring of literature and art has arrived.

In December of last year, the Eleventh Central Committee held its third plenary session, calling on the entire Party and nation to shift the focus of its work to socialist modernization. The third plenary session highly esteemed the discussion on the criteria for truth that had developed throughout the country and set forth the guiding principles of "emancipating thought, setting machines in motion, seeking truth from facts, and uniting together to look toward the future." Presently, the people of the entire nation, under the leadership of the Party Central Committee, are waging a great struggle to realize the Four Modernizations. Writers and artists must stand in the forefront of this struggle. For the past three years, major achievements have been attained on the fronts of literature and art, but these fall far short of satisfying the needs of the broad masses. How to further unleash the power of literary and artistic production, bring about the prosperity of socialist literature and art, and better serve the Four Modernizations is the battle cry raised to us by the Party and the people; it is a matter of great concern to comrades in literary and art circles, and the major topic to be discussed at this meeting.

According to the resolution of the Third Expanded Session of the Chinese Federation of Literary and Art Circles, the task of this present meeting is "to sum up the abundant positive and negative experiences on the literature and art fronts since the founding of our nation, to discuss the tasks and plans of literary and artistic work in this new period, to revise the bylaws of the Chinese Federation of Literary and Art Circles and other associations, and to elect the leadership of these organizations." As we convene this meeting, each association is about to separately convene its delegate assembly. Through this congress and these assemblies, we must promote new literary and artistic developments and initiate a new era in which socialist literature and art will flourish. Only by upholding the policy of "letting a hundred flowers bloom and a hundred schools of thought contend" can we create even more and better works of literature and art and make the necessary contributions to the socialist cause, the worldwide struggle against imperialism and hegemonism, and the development of progressive culture.

Comrades, we must adhere to the instructions of Marxism-Leninism—Mao Zedong Thought pertaining to work in the fields of literature and art. Marxism-Leninism and Mao Zedong Thought are sciences that guide practice, not dogmas. We are facing new historical conditions that our revolutionary teachers did not encounter in their lives. Real life has posed a series of new questions for literary and artistic work. Practice is the sole criterion for determining truth. We must seek answers to these new questions through repeated practice.

Comrades, our strength lies in unity. Through this congress, we must move further toward promoting solidarity among literary and art circles. This congress must be a unified meeting that emancipates thought and fosters democracy. I hope that everyone will be able to speak freely about the central topics of this meeting and the matters that concern us. We must continue to deeply criticize the ultra-leftist line of Lin Biao and the Gang of Four in order to eliminate its pernicious influence. When we hold different opinions concerning matters of literary and artistic thought, we must not take violent measures, for this not only harms solidarity but also hinders the development of literature and art. We must strengthen the unity between the leaders and the led as well as the unity between Party and non-Party, old and new, and professional and amateur writers and artists. We serve the broad masses. Our task is to work for the realization of the Four Modernizations. In order to attain this lofty goal, we must unite even more closely so that our cause will achieve still greater victories.

Comrades, our congress proclaims that the new Long March in socialist literature and art has already begun and it possesses great significance in the history of literature and art. The writers, artists, and masses of the nation are placing their fervent hopes in this congress; our international friends are also following this meeting with interest. I firmly believe that through the concerted efforts of all the delegates the accomplishments of our congress will be most fruitful. Let us unite closely and strive together to make socialist literature and art flourish even more.

Translated by Wendy Locks
(Wenyibao, 1979, Nos. 11–12)

2

CONGRATULATORY MESSAGE TO THE FOURTH CONGRESS OF CHINESE WRITERS AND ARTISTS

Deng Xiaoping

Delegates and Comrades:

Today, delegates of writers, playwrights, artists, musicians, performing artists, film workers, and other workers in the field of literature and the arts from all over China are happily gathered in this hall. You are here to review your experiences in the last three decades, to enhance your achievements, to overcome all your short-comings, and to find ways to promote literature and art in this new historic period. This is indeed an epoch-making event. On behalf of the Central Committee of the Chinese Communist Party and the State Council, I would like to extend my warm greetings to you.

Among all the distinguished delegates present in this hall, some are veteran writers and artists who joined the New Culture Move-ment during the May Fourth period; others have made contributions to our people's liberation during the various stages of our revolu-tionary struggle following the May Fourth Movement; some have grown up after the founding of the People's Republic; and still others appeared during our struggle against Lin Biao and the Gang of Four. Our meeting is attended by writers and artists from Taiwan, Hong Kong, and Macao. This congress symbolizes an unprecedented unity among Chinese writers and artists.

Our policy on literature and art was on the right course and our achievements in this area were remarkable during the seventeen years prior to the Cultural Revolution. The so-called "black-line dictatorship" was a total calumny fabricated by Lin Biao and the Gang of Four. A great many brilliant literary and art works were banned and a large number of literary and art workers were wronged and persecuted during the ten years that Lin Biao and the Gang of Four were on their rebellious rampage. During those trying times, many of our friends and comrades in the literary and art fields firmly and steadfastly resisted and struggled against Lin Biao and the Gang of Four. In this victorious struggle by the Party and the people, literary and art workers made admirable and unforgettable contributions, and I want to take this opportunity to express my warm regards to you all.

Since the smashing of the Gang of Four, under the leadership of the Party Central Committee, the Party's policy concerning intellectuals has been implemented and many literary and art works that were earlier welcomed by the people have been republished. With high spirits and relaxed minds, our literary and art workers are enthusiastically engaging in their creative work. Through a thorough repudiation and exposure of the ultra-leftist line of Lin Biao and the Gang of Four, many excellent novels, poems, dramas, films, examples of folk art, and reportage, as well as music, dance, photographs, and other art works have been produced over the last couple of years. These works have played an active role in smashing the spiritual shackles put into place by Lin Biao and the Gang of Four and eradicating their noxious influence; they have also helped to emanciplate the people's thought and have promoted unity among the people in working together for the Four Modernizations. In my judgment, during the three years since the smashing of the Gang of Four, literature and art is one of the fields in which excellent results have been achieved. Our writers and artists, therefore, deserve the trust, love, and respect of both the Party and the people. Our contingent of literary and art workers has been rigorously tested by struggles in this stormy period, and, in general, they have proved themselves worthy of the task. The Party and the people are very pleased to have such writers and artists.

Delegates and Comrades:

Our motherland has entered a new era of socialist modernization. As we try to increase our socialist productivity at a much faster rate, we should simultaneously try to improve and reform the socialist economic and political systems, develop a much higher level of socialist democracy, and establish an adequate legal system. While we are trying to construct a more elevated material civilization, we should also try to raise the scientific and cultural levels of our people and develop an elegant, rich, and colorful cultural life, thus building a highly socialistic spiritual civilization.

The completion of the Four Modernizations will be the top priority of our people for a very long time to come, to which we should all dedicate our minds and souls. The destiny of our country depends on this great undertaking. The masses and cadres on all fronts should serve as activists in emancipating thought, promoting stability and unity, defending the unification of our motherland, and accomplishing the Four Modernizations. The sole criterion for deciding the correctness of all work should be whether that work is helpful or harmful to the accomplishment of the Four Modernizations. Our literary and art workers should cooperate with workers in the fields of education, philosophy, journalism, politics, and other related areas in waging a protracted and effective ideological struggle against ideas and habits that may hinder the accomplishment of the Four Modernizations. We must criticize the ideas of the exploiting classes, the influences of conservatism, and the narrow-minded, small-producer mentality, as well as anarchism, extreme individualism, and bureaucracy. It is imperative for us to restore and expand the revolutionary traditions of our Party and the people, cultivate fine morality and social customs, and make positive contributions to a highly developed socialist spiritual civilization.

In this great undertaking, there is ample room for us to promote literature and art. Literature and art occupy a pivotal position, which can help to satisfy the people's spiritual needs, educate new socialist youth, and raise the ideological, cultural, and moral levels of the entire society. This important responsibility cannot be assumed by any other sector. Our literature and art belong to the people. Our people are industrious, brave, determined, and unshakable. They are wise and full of high ideals. They love our motherland and socialism and are well-disciplined and unselfish. In the past thousands of years, particularly in the half-century following the May Fourth Movement, they have displayed remarkable confidence by struggling through storms and overcoming all kinds of obstacles. Their brilliant deeds have filled chapter after chapter of Chinese history. No enemies, no matter how powerful, have ever been able to conquer them; no difficulties, no matter how serious, have ever been able to stop them. Writers and artists have to make sure that they describe and praise the fine qualities of our people and the great victories they have won in the course of our revolution and construction, as well as their struggles against various enemies and difficulties.

Our writers and artists should make every effort to attain even greater achievements in describing and promoting our new socialist youth. Writers and artists should portray pioneers in the Four Modernizations drive. They should vividly depict the pioneers' revolutionary ideals and scientific approaches, their noble sentiments and creations, their great vision, and their down-to-earth attitude. Writers and artists should use the pioneers' new images to whip up enthusiasm for socialism among our masses, encouraging them to embark upon the epochal mission of the Four Modernizations.

Our socialist literature and art should vividly describe the inner and essential qualities of our people in their social relations, give expression to the trend of historical development and our people's desire for progress, educate them in socialist ideology, and imbue them with the determination to strive for a brighter future.

Our country has a very long history, a vast area, and a huge population. China is made up of people from different nationalities, occupations, ages, experience, and educational backgrounds. They have different habits, cultural heritages, and artistic aptitudes and preferences. Any literary and artistic work that provides education as well as enlightenment, and at the same time gives the people entertainment and esthetic enjoyment, regardless of its scope or whether it is serious, humorous, or philosophical, should have a place in our literature and art. Creative works should portray feats of heroism as well as daily labor and the struggles, joys, and sorrows of ordinary people; their themes can be either modern or ancient. The best of all ages and countries should be critically assimilated.

We must adhere to Comrade Mao Zedong's principle that art and literature should serve the people, particularly the worker-peasant-soldier masses, and follow his policies of "letting a hundred flowers bloom," "weeding out the old to bring forth the new," and "making foreign and ancient things serve China." The unhampered development of different styles in creative works and free discussion of divergent viewpoints and schools of thought in literary and art theories should all be encouraged. Lenin once said: "[In literature] it is absolutely necessary to guarantee that writers have ample room for individual creation and inclination, and ample room for different ideas, imagination, forms, and contents." Geared to reach the common goal of realizing the Four Modernizations, writers and artists should broaden the horizons of their work; their creative thinking, themes, and techniques should change and adapt to time and tide, and should be able to plow new ground. Writers and artists should prevent and overcome the tendency of monotonous formulism and jargonism.

Recognizing their responsibilities to the people, writers and artists should consider the social effect of their works. They should at all times adjust their works to the needs of the masses, work diligently to improve, and take every precaution against producing shabby work; rather they should provide the people with food for thought. Lin Biao and the Gang of Four, before their downfall, corrupted people's souls with their reactionary, decadent ideology of the exploiting class and poisoned our social environment. They seriously undermined our revolutionary tradition and our treasured revolutionary heritage. Writers and artists should, through their creative work, elevate the minds of the masses to a higher spiritual plateau and continue to wage an unyielding struggle against the malignant influence of Lin Biao and the Gang of Four. Writers and artists should be on guard against pressure from the "Left" as well as the "Right" to stir up social unrest and disrupt political stability and unity. These erroneous tendencies run counter to the interests and wishes of the majority of our people. Writers and artists should unite with others in the ideological field to alert the people to these dangers and condemn them.

Literary and art workers should exert themselves in the study of Marxism-Leninism—Mao Zedong Thought. They should try to enhance their ability to comprehend and analyze life as well as their ability to seize the real meaning of things through reality. We sincerely hope that more and more comrades among our literary and art workers will become the de facto "engineers of the human soul." Those who wish to educate others must first of all educate themselves. Those who give nourishment must first absorb nourishment themselves. The question is, "Who should be the ones to educate and nourish our literary and art workers?" The answer provided by Marxism is simple enough: the people. The people are the mother of literary and art workers. All progressive literary and art workers owe their creative lives to their flesh-and-blood relationship with the people. Forgetting, neglecting, or severing this relationship would eventually dry up one's creative life. The people need art, but art needs people even more. Our writers and artists should conscientiously draw their raw materials, themes, plots, language, poetic diction and sentiment, and picturesque meaning from the people's daily experiences, then nurture themselves in the history-making, hardworking spirit of the people.

This is the only course that will make our socialist literature and art flourish and prosper. We are confident that our writers and artists will unswervingly follow this course as they move forward.

Writers and artists should continue to enrich and elevate their talents in artistic expression. They should earnestly study, assimilate, apply, and develop all the fine artistic skills and techniques, domestic and foreign. Then and only then will they be able to create faultless artistic forms with a unique national character and the spirit of the times. Only those writers and artists who dare to confront difficulties, who study and practice diligently, and who are brave in exploring new ground can hope to scale the artistic heights.

It is our sincere wish that our literary and art contingent will become more united and will grow stronger day by day. All of our writers and artists, whether professional or amateur, socialist or patriotic, as long as they support the unification of our motherland, should strive to assist and learn from each other. They should devote all their energy to literary and artistic creation, research, and criticism. It is completely up to the people to appraise and evaluate the literary and artistic achievements of our writers and artists, be it on ideological or artistic planes. The driving force behind the artists' progress and improvement is their ability to heed and accept constructive criticism and suggestions. Within the literary and art contingent, there should be comradely and friendly give-and-take discussions among writers of different genres and artists of different forms, among creative writers and literary critics, and between writers and artists and their readers and audiences. They should present facts and settle disputes by reasoning. Criticism and counter-criticism must be tolerated. Writers and artists should always uphold the truth and correct their mistakes whenever necessary.

It is a very important task for the veteran writers and artists to discover and train their younger counterparts. Young writers and artists are full of energy and their minds are sharp; they comprise our literary and artistic heritage. We should, on the one hand, zealously help them, and, on the other hand, set rigorous demands for them to meet so that they will not deviate from real life and will make continuous ideological as well as artistic progress. Middle-aged writers and artists are the backbone of our literary and art contingent. Their talents should be fully utilized.

We must pay more attention to the training of literary and artistic talents. In a huge country such as ours, with a population of

more than 900 million, there are far too few first-rate writers and
artists. This condition is quite unsuitable to our needs at the present time. We must not only create the essential ideological conditions, but also improve our own system so as to make the introduction and cultivation of outstanding talents possible. Our Party committees at all levels must exercise cogent leadership in literature
and art. This leadership should not be realized by issuing administrative orders or presenting demands that literature and art be subordinate to a temporary, specific, and direct political assignment.
Rather, the Party committees should, based upon the characteristics
of literature and art and the laws of development, help writers and
artists meet the conditions for making literary and artistic undertakings flourish, elevate literary and art levels, and create excellent literary and art works; they should also promote the development of performing skills worthy of our great people and our great
era. At this point in time, we should make every effort to help
writers and artists continue to emancipate their thought and smash
the spiritual shackles put into place by Lin Biao and the Gang of
Four. We should, at the same time, help them to maintain a correct
political orientation, and strive to support them in every respect,
materially or otherwise, to ensure that they can fully utilize their
wisdom and talents. We urge literary and artistic leaders to exchange opinions with writers and artists as equals. By the same
token, writers and artists who are Party members should use their
own achievements to play an exemplary role in attracting and
uniting the broad masses of writers and artists, as they move forward together. The issuing of executive orders in the areas of literary and artistic creation and criticism must be stopped. If we
view such things as upholding Party leadership, the results will be
the opposite of that intended. We must uphold the ideological line
of dialectical materialism and must analyze the positive as well as
negative experiences learned in the history of literary and artistic
development over the last thirty years. We must shake off all the
yokes of outmoded ideas and dogmas. We must study new situations
and solve fresh problems according to the characteristics of our
new era. The ludicrous policies advocated by Lin Biao and the Gang
of Four not only undermined our Party leadership over literary and
art work but also suffocated literary and artistic life. In mental
endeavors as complicated as literature and art, it is absolutely essential for writers and artists to totally utilize their individual
creative spirit. Writers and artists must have the freedom to

choose their subject matter and method of presentation based upon artistic practice and exploration. No interference in this regard can be permitted.

Delegates and Comrades:

Comrade Mao Zedong pointed out at the founding of our People's Republic of China: "As soon as our economic construction reaches its peak, our cultural construction will naturally follow suit." Through strenuous struggle and by overcoming all kinds of difficulties, we have smashed the Gang of Four, thus wiping out the major obstacle that stood in our way. At present, we can proclaim with full confidence that what Comrade Mao said will soon come true; conditions for putting into practice the Marxist principle of "letting a hundred flowers bloom and a hundred schools of thought contend" improve daily. Through the hard-working efforts of writers and artists, a new era of literary and artistic prosperity will soon be upon us.

This congress is the first important gathering of writers and artists from all over China in our new Long March of Modernization. Those who are assembled here have brought with them their laudable achievements. We firmly believe that after this congress our comrades will surely produce many more and much better creative works to share with our fellow countrymen.

I wish this congress great success.

Translated by George Cheng
(Wenyibao, 1979, Nos. 11–12)

3

INHERIT THE PAST AND USHER IN THE FUTURE

Zhou Yang

The Fourth Congress of Chinese Writers and Artists is being held as we celebrate the thirtieth anniversary of the People's Republic of China. It has been exactly thirty years since the First Congress of Writers and Artists and nineteen years since the Third Congress....

After ten years of chaos and deep suffering caused by Lin Biao and the Gang of Four,...our country has now moved into a new period of socialist modernization.... This meeting will go down in China's history of socialist literature and art as one of special importance. It marks the end of the feudal-fascist dictatorship of Lin Biao and the Gang of Four and the beginning of a new period....

A COURSE OF HARD STRUGGLE

. . . .

China's socialist literature and art, like her work in all other fields, have gone through a great and arduous course in the thirty years of the People's Republic. We have made great achievements and gained a wealth of experience both positive and negative.

[The idea of] socialist literature and art was born more than a hundred years ago in the time of Marx and Engels. It did not come into existence peacefully but through fierce struggles. Because of the great October Revolution, the literature of Soviet Russia became the vanguard of world socialist literature and art. China's new literature and art first followed the examples of Russia, northern and southeastern Europe, and the Soviet Union. Lu Xun's Call to Arms and Guo Moruo's The Goddesses, which appeared during the May Fourth New Culture Movement, laid a solid foundation for a new kind of essay and poetry. The period from the "revolution in liter-

ature" of the May Fourth Movement to the "revolutionary literature"
of the Great Revolution of 1924–27 was a time of a "leap forward"
in Chinese literary history.

In the thirties the movement of left-wing literature and art, under
the leadership of the Chinese Communist Party and with the great
Lu Xun as the standard-bearer, raised the banner of a proletarian
literature. This movement defeated the counterrevolutionary cultural "encirclement and annihilation" of the Guomindang [KMT] reactionaries and, with the blood of revolutionary writers and artists,
wrote a new chapter in China's proletarian literature and art. The
deaths of Rou Shi, Hu Yepin, and three other martyrs in the thirties and
Wen Yiduo in the forties, all at the hands of the Guomindang reactionaries, were examples of writers giving their lives for the truth.

The revolutionary literature and art of the thirties, with their
fierce, militant spirit, inspired the broad masses of the people suffering under national and class oppression and thus contributed in-
delibly to the New Democratic Revolution against imperialism and
feudalism and to the victory of the war for national liberation.
Some of the most widely acclaimed works of the time included Lu
Xun's militant essays and other works, Mao Dun's Midnight and
other novels, Ye Shaojun's Ni Huanzhi, Ba Jin's Family, Cao Yu's
Thunderstorm, Lao She's Camel Xiangzi [Ricksha Boy], and Li
Jieren's Still Waters and Gentle Waves. The literary and dramatic
works of Tien Han, Xia Yan, Jiang Guangci, Zhang Tianyi, and many
other revolutionary writers spread revolutionary thinking among
the people and the young intellectuals. Bound Labor, as the first
reportage describing the plight of China's industrial workers, broke
fresh ground in this genre. The new woodcuts promoted and fostered by Lu Xun were an important part of the left-wing literature
and art movement. Musical and dramatic activities that inspired
and mobilized the people in the fight to save the country from Japanese aggression included choral and dramatic performances, such
as the song "March of the Volunteers" and the skit Put Down Your
Whip!

Young writers from the Japanese-occupied Northeast became an
important voice in literature when they wrote about the sufferings
and resistance of the thirty million people living under enemy occu-
pation. The struggles of the time were faithfully recorded in the
novels Village in August and The Field of Life and Death. There
were also creative and mass cultural activities in the revolutionary
bases of Jiangxi and northern Shaanxi provinces.

The proletarian literature and art of this period, appearing for the first time in Chinese history, were of course still in their infancy. Most of the works were ideologically and artistically immature. Many writers were not yet free from petty bourgeois influence. Activists in the left-wing literature and art movement like Qu Qiubai, Yang Hansheng, Feng Xuefeng, and Ah Ying worked assiduously to propagate Marxist literary and artistic theory and organize the left-wing ranks. But because we did not have a good grasp of Marxist theory, an in-depth understanding of the realities of the Chinese revolution, or sufficient historical knowledge and social experience, we developed a tendency toward dogmatism and factionalism in varying degrees, even as we were propagating Marxist theories and learning from the experience of international proletarian revolutionary literature and art movements. ...

Comrade Mao Zedong's "Talks at the Yan'an Forum on Literature and Art," delivered in 1942, was an epochal document in the history of Chinese literature and art. In clear-cut language, "Talks" put forth the idea that literature and art must serve the workers, peasants, and soldiers and the broad masses of the people, that writers and artists must integrate themselves with the masses of a new age. "Talks" thus correctly solved a fundamental theoretical question, namely, Whom should literature and art serve and how to serve them? This brought about tremendous changes in both the content and the form of our revolutionary literature and art. Before and after "Talks," writers and artists in the revolutionary bases went among the workers, peasants, and soldiers and integrated themselves with these people. They paid serious attention to folk art and the new creative works of the people and were in turn greatly influenced by the people's thoughts and feelings and esthetic views. Representative works described the revolutionary changes in this new period and gave a totally new look to literature and art. Among the works were the new yangge skit Sister and Brother Reclaim the Wasteland, the new-style opera The White-haired Girl, the new Peking opera Driven up the Liangshan Mountains, the new Shaanxi-style opera Revenge, the new folk song The East Is Red, as well as The Yellow River Cantata, March of the Eighth Route Army, and Song of the Guerrillas, the new woodcuts and new-year pictures, the ballads Guards along the Border Area and Wang Gui and Li Xiangxiang, the novelette The Rhymes of Li Youcai, and the novels The Sun Shines over the Sanggan River, The Hurricane, Uncle Gao, and Unwithering Flowers. ...

In the Guomindang areas, revolutionary and progressive writers and artists created a host of fine works. Important ones included the long poems The Torch and To the Militants, the novel The Gold-diggers, the stage plays Before and After Qing Ming, Fascist Bacillus, and Foggy Chongqing. Guo Moruo's historical stage play Qu Yuan created a sensation when it denounced the Kuomintang reactionaries in historical allegory....

The First Congress of Writers and Artists, held in Peking in 1949, was a great joining of forces of two contingents of revolutionary writers and artists, one from the old liberated areas and one from the former Guomindang areas. The meeting was held after the Communist Party had won political power throughout the country, after we had moved from a war environment to peacetime construction, from the countryside to the cities.... The founding of the People's Republic of China marked the conclusion of the New Democratic Revolution and the beginning of the Socialist Revolution. It marked the establishment of the people's democratic dictatorship, that is, the dictatorship of the proletariat, throughout the country. This presented us with new tasks, namely, how to make literature and art, as a form of ideology, suit a socialist economic base, how to depict the many facets of the new life and struggle and the new thoughts and feelings of the people in this new historical period, and how to satisfy the people's growing need for a diverse cultural life....

After the founding of the People's Republic, under the leadership of the Party Central Committee and Comrade Mao Zedong, a series of large-scale criticisms against bourgeois and feudal ideas was carried out in literary and art circles. These were the criticism of the film Life of Wu Xun, the criticism of the subjective idealism of Hu Shi and his followers in the critical study of the classical novel A Dream of Red Mansions, and the criticism of the political and artistic viewpoints of Hu Feng. As ideological and artistic criticisms, these were necessary and important struggles. But to conduct them as political movements on a nationwide scale, as these were, produced some serious negative results. China at the time had entered the socialist period. Socialist transformation was an extremely profound process of change aimed at eliminating private ownership of the means of production. Socialist economy and politics require a compatible socialist ideology. Since bourgeois and feudal ideas had been deep-rooted, struggles in all aspects of ideology were inevitable. We had to use Marxism as a weapon to de-

feat all kinds of exploiting-class ideology so that proletarian ideology would hold sway. With the conclusion of the struggles mentioned above, and after socialist transformation was realized in the
main in 1956, the Party Central Committee and Comrade Mao Zedong put forth the policy of "letting a hundred flowers bloom and a
hundred schools of thought contend" — a policy of enormous significance for developing a socialist literature and art.

Right after the founding of the new China, we faced the problem
of how to handle our traditional operas, which included Peking opera
and the many local styles of opera.... Operatic dramas constituted
an extremely rich and valuable legacy the people had created over
a long period of time; still they were the products of the old days
and contained many harmful feudal ideas as well as fine elements
of a democratic nature. Reform was called for. In accordance with
Comrade Mao Zedong's proposal, and working together with operatic artists, we proceeded to sort out and reform traditional repertoires and the art of performance according to three categories:
beneficial, harmless, and harmful. The results: many operatic
styles that had been on the verge of extinction were given a new
lease on life, and the scripts and singing styles of a host of traditional operas shone forth with new brilliance....

In the first seventeen years of Liberation, fine operas were the
mainstream on the operatic stage, even though some undesirable
ones also appeared. In both Peking opera and local-style operas,
there had appeared many good works rich in innovative spirit and
artistic power, such as Reconciliation of the General and the Prime
Minister, Liang Shanbo and Zhu Yingtai, The White Snake, The Tale
of Fu Nu, Fifteen Strings of Cash, Women Generals of the Yang
Family, Tablet of Life and Death, Sparks amid the Reeds, The Red
Lantern, Jie Zhenguo, The Young Husband, Liu Qiao-er, Heavenly
Match, Searching the Academy, Defeating the White Bone Demon,
and Chaoyang Ditch. Especially important was the reform of the
traditional opera to make it a vehicle for the expression of contemporary life. The 1964 festival of modern revolutionary Peking opera
was a review of these achievements....

New China devoted great efforts toward developing the motion
picture industry. Back in the thirties, left-wing film workers, under the leadership of the Communist Party and resisting the heavy
pressures of the Guomindang reactionaries, pioneered the cause of
revolutionary motion pictures. Fine films still fresh in people's
memories include The Fishing People, Plight of Youth, Lights of

Ten Thousand Families, Crows and Sparrows, and The River Flows
East.

With nationwide Liberation the motion picture industry made unprecedented developments. Film after film showed the viewers a
new world and new people. The most popular ones included Daugh-
ters of China, Man of Steel, The White-haired Girl, Red Flags over
Green Hills, Dong Cunrui, Red Detachment of Women, Locust Village, Li Shuangshuang, The Undying Wavelength, Sangkumryung, The
Storm, New Tales of an Old Soldier, Lin Zexu, The Storm of 1894,
New Year Sacrifice, Waves Washing the Sands, The Serf, City under
Siege, Stage Sisters, Early Spring, and Heroic Son and Daughter....

Vigorous development in literature in the first seventeen years
of Liberation can be seen in a host of popular novels, plays, poetry,
and essays.... Lao She's ...plays Dragon Beard Ditch and Tea-
house both portray the life of the people of Peking with whom he
was so familiar. With profound yet succinct depiction he exposes
the darkness of old China and praises the new regime of the people.
Guo Moruo's Cai Wenji and Tian Han's Guan Hanqing and Princess
Wencheng all present historical figures in a new light and introduce new viewpoints in portraying relations between the Han and
the minority peoples. As such the plays are an expression of the
artistic courage and searching spirit of the veteran writers. Historical and present-day struggles are depicted in the stage plays
Maturing in Fighting, Across Mountains and Rivers, Sentries under
the Neon Lights, and Never Forget, and in the new-style operas Red
Guards of Lake Hunghu, The Marriage of Xiao Erhei, Liu Hulan,
Red Coral, Sister Jiang, and Third Sister Liu. The people's revolutionary struggles of the preceding half-century are also re-cre-
ated in the novels The Builders, Keep the Red Flag Flying, Red
Crag, Song of Youth, Winds and Clouds, Tracks in the Snowy For-
est, Struggles in a Small City, Three-Family Lane, Great Changes
in a Mountain Village, Red Sun, Railroad Guerrillas, Bitter Flow-
ers, Defend Yan'an, Wall of Bronze, Motive Force, Steeled and
Tempered, Militant Youth, Morning in Shanghai, Goldsand Bar,
Fragrant through the Seasons, Wind and Thunder, The Song of
Ouyang Hai, and Li Zicheng and in the short-story anthologies
Political Commissar, Three Thousand Li of Mountains and Rivers,
The Night of the Snowstorm, Dawn over the River, Party Fee, Lilies
of the Valley, The Story of Li Shuangshuang, My First Superior Of-
ficer, Spring Sowing and Autumn Harvest. The reportage Who
Are the Most Lovable People? moves the reader with a strong in-

ternational spirit. The Story of Luo Wenying has also won the hearts
of young readers. The short story "The Young Newcomer from the
Organization Department" and the reportage "On the Bridge Site,"
which deal with the contradictions among the people in the socialist
period with bold, incisive description, are fine examples of the
critical role of literature and have aroused serious attention from
readers....

New works of painting, sculpture, music, and dance experimented
with developing a national and popular style. Representative works
are the paintings Inauguration Ceremony, How Beautiful Are the
Rivers and Mountains, and Blood-stained Coat, the bas-relief frieze
on the Monument to the People's Heroes, the group sculpture Rent
Collection Yard, the music and dance epic The East Is Red, the
choral suite The Long March, the symphonic poem Gadamirin, the
dance dramas Small Swords Society and Red Detachment of Wom-
en....

In their scheme to seize supreme power in the Party and the
state, Lin Biao and the Gang of Four began with seizing power in
literary and art circles. They began by slandering the historical
play Hai Rui Dismissed from Office. The so-called Summary of the
Forum on Literary and Art Work in the Armed Forces was the sig-
nal to implement their overall seizure of power and their program
to exercise "overall dictatorship" in literature and art. They
usurped Party leadership over literary and art work and held it for
nearly a decade. With this power they pushed a most reactionary
cultural policy and practiced feudal-fascist cultural autocracy and
cultural nihilism to make the decade the darkest period in the cultural history of the new China. They tried to write off not only all
the literary and artistic achievements of the first seventeen years
of Liberation, but also the great achievements and glorious traditions of revolutionary literature and art since the thirties and even
as far back as the May Fourth Movement of 1919. They said that
our socialist literature and art had followed an "anti-Party and
anti-socialist black line." They called revolutionary writers and
artists "black-line figures" and called Party leadership in literary
and art work a "dictatorship of the black line." They banned all
fine works past and present, Chinese and foreign, trying to write
off all the progressive culture of mankind. The Chinese Federation of
Literary and Art Circles and its affiliate associations were slan-
dered as "Petofi Clubs" and were forced to disband. Huge numbers
of writers and artists were persecuted and humiliated. It was in

all an unprecedented holocaust for socialist literature and art....

The Gang of Four pushed the ultra-left line as part of their scheme to usurp total Party power. They distorted Comrade Mao Zedong's ideas on literature and art. They severed the ties between the people and the arts and denied the fact that social life was the only source for literary and artistic creation. They substituted lies and falsehoods for the realities of life and true art, severely damaging the reputation of revolutionary literature and art. They distorted the correct relationship between politics and the arts. They enslaved the arts with counterrevolutionary politics, turning the arts into tools for conspiracy and slaves of reactionary politics. They spread what they called the theories of the "three prominences" and "the theme leading the way." They stultified literary and artistic styles. These plus a series of absurd measures made a mess of the Party's work in literature and art. The harmful influence was so great that much still needs to be done to clear it away entirely.

From the historical point of view, however, the interference and disruption of Lin Biao and the Gang of Four were short-lived. They did not and could not completely halt the development of socialist literature and art. Most of the writers and artists did not knuckle under to the tyranny of the Gang of Four. Openly or in devious and covert ways they fought back.... Their struggle against Lin Biao and the Gang of Four was a struggle between the revolutionary people and the counterrevolutionary conspirators-careerists, between the Party's policy of "letting a hundred flowers bloom and a hundred schools of thought contend" and feudal-fascist cultural autocracy and cultural nihilism, between dialectical materialism and subjective idealism, between revolutionary realism and formulism-jargonism. It was an intense struggle, Many writers and artists, though in adverse circumstances, continued to conceive new works or actually write them down in secret.... After undergoing severe tests, our ranks of writers and artists, except for a very small number of scum and opportunists, have proved to be an indestructible battalion....

In the three years following the overthrow of the Gang of Four, especially in the last year or two, writers and artists have criticized and repudiated the many falsehoods spread by Lin Biao and the Gang of Four, including "the dictatorship of the black line in literature and art." The policies for literature and art formulated by the Party Central Committee and Comrade Mao Zedong have once more been correctly interpreted and earnestly implemented. Our socialist literature and art have begun to revive and make progress. The spirit of the Third Plenary Session of the Eleventh Party Central Committee and the discussion on the criterion of truth have led to a great emancipation of thought. As soon as the Gang of Four fell, cartoons and comic dialogues came out with stinging satires directed at the enemy. Revolutionary poems and poetry recitation, breaking long years of silence, expressed the people's militant feelings. Especially worth mentioning are the widely read Poems from Tian An Men and new poems by veteran and young poets eulogizing the heroic people and denouncing the Gang of Four....

Questions that writers and artists had not dared touch for a long time are now being probed and discussed. Not only the taboos imposed on writers and artists by the Gang of Four but many restrictions of the first seventeen years are being challenged and discarded. Literary and artistic works of all forms have mushroomed. Much acclaimed works include the novelettes and short stories "The Class Counsellor," "My Sacred Duty," "The Window," "Our Army Commander," "The Wounded," "Manager Qiao Assumes Office," "The Blood-stained Magnolia," and "The Path Through the Grassland"; the special feature "Between Men and Monsters"; the plays Loyal Hearts, In a Silent Place, May Youth Be More Beautiful, The Future Beckons, and Azalea; and the opera Oh, Starlight! The newest dance drama Along the Silk Road, with its fresh and richly Chinese style, praises the friendship between the Chinese and foreign peoples of ancient times and the unyielding struggles and creative spirit of the workingman artists. Stage plays such as Paperboys, Dawn, and Chen Yi Comes out of the Mountains are attempts at portraying veteran revolutionary leaders. New works by veteran writers include the novel about the Korean war The East, the historical stage plays Wang Zhaojun and Song of the Great Wind, and the reportage on the scientist of today Goldbach Conjecture. New subjects and new treatment in motion pictures are represented by [the films] From Slave to General, Ji Hongchang, and Xiao Hua....

The murals in the new Capital Airport [Peking], which won high acclaim at home and abroad, are blazing a new trail in this form of art....

Following the realist tradition of socialist literature and art, many works in this period, short stories and stage plays initially,

describe the intense struggles between the people and the Gang of
Four and the complex social contradictions of those dark days.
Many portray veteran revolutionaries and advanced people on the
new Long March, or expose the obstructions and malpractices that
hinder the effort to modernize the country. While the subjects are
varied, all pose urgent problems in real life and, as such, reflect
the people's wishes, ideals, moods, and demands. They are an out-
come of the current movement to emancipate thought and have in
turn given fresh impetus to this movement. Many of these works
are by young writers who recount their own experiences and feelings. With keen observation and a bold, searching spirit, they accuse, protest, and cry out, because their experience has been filled
with bitterness, sorrow, indignation, and grief. Some write about
their awakening and struggles after seeing through the frauds.
Casting aside taboos and conventions, and with trenchant style, they
describe their innermost feelings and the shocking incidents they
have witnessed or heard. Their works reflect the deep spiritual
wounds Lin Biao and the Gang of Four inflicted on the people and
expose their towering crimes. We should not casually censure these
works as "literature of the wounded" or "exposé literature." The
people's spiritual wounds and the counterrevolutionary gang that
inflicted those wounds are all facts. How can our writers cover
them up or whitewash them? How can writers close their eyes to
the contradictions in real life? Of course we do not condone describing the spiritual wounds in a naturalistic way that will lead to
negative, apathetic, and nihilistic thoughts and feelings. The people
need healthy literature and art. We need the power of literature and
art to help people better understand their bitter experience, heal
their wounds, and learn their lessons so that the same tragedies
will not happen again.

Coming from the people, these works have the rich flavor of life
and the spirit of the times. Most of the authors are newcomers,
often immature, who have shortcomings. It is only normal that
there are differing views regarding some of these works. We
should allow free discussion and debates, while the authors should
keep an open mind and lend their ears to the different views. In any
case, the new writers are pondering, working, making progress.
They represent the younger generation in Chinese literature; they
are in the process of maturing. They have unlimited potential, so
we should welcome them, encourage them, and guide them. Our
literature and art should promote unity, not disunity, among the

people. They should inspire people to look forward, not make them feel discouraged. They should broaden the people's horizons, not make them shortsighted. All works that corrode the soul and corrupt social mores should be criticized and repudiated.

For the greater part of the past thirty years, except for the ten years of holocaust under Lin Biao and the Gang of Four, our work in literature and art has basically implemented the line defined by the Party and Comrade Mao Zedong and, generally speaking, has been guided by Marxism-Leninism–Mao Zedong Thought. Mao Zedong's thinking on literature and art, which is an important part of Mao Zedong Thought, has educated generation after generation of our writers and artists. Comrade Zhou Enlai was exemplary in applying this thinking to practice. He and Comrade Chen Yi gave many talks explaining the tremendous importance of practicing democracy in promoting a socialist literature and art. Thanks to their guidance, the 1961 meeting on motion pictures, held in the Xinqiao Hotel in Peking, and the 1962 meeting on drama, held in Guangzhou, were both successful. In 1962, in view of the shortcomings and mistakes that had appeared for a period of time in our work, the Party committees of the Ministry of Culture and the Federation of Literary and Art Circles proposed ways for improving literary and artistic work (proposals known as "The Eight Points on Literary and Art Work"). These proposals were basically correct.

Unquestionably, in literature and art our achievements have been primary and enormous; the mainstream has been correct and healthy. But we must also admit that there have been many shortcomings and mistakes. A "leftist" tendency in our guiding thought has been particularly harmful. Lin Biao and the Gang of Four, while slandering the correct line we followed as a counterrevolutionary revisionist line, made use of our "leftist" shortcomings and mistakes and carried them to the ultra-left extreme. While our "leftist" mistakes were fundamentally different in nature from the ultra-left line Lin Biao and the Gang of Four pursued in their attempt to usurp Party power, we cannot excuse ourselves for our mistakes simply because of the interruption and disruption of Lin Biao and the Gang of Four. We should fully affirm our achievements while facing up to our shortcomings and mistakes. We must be prepared to learn a lesson from our agonizing experience to be on guard for what the future brings.

Owing to the particular conditions of the times and our failure

to overcome our "leftist" tendencies, some of us in the literary and
artistic leadership were at times unable to correctly and realistically appraise the situation of class struggle in the literary and art
fields and thus failed to correctly handle the relationship between
politics and the arts. We carried out class struggle on a much
wider scale than was actually called for and confused the contradictions between the enemy and the people with the contradictions
among the people themselves. Consequently we handled criticisms
of ideology, of literary and artistic ideas, as if they were political
movements and used the method of mass struggle to handle questions belonging in the spiritual realm. This brought injury to a
number of comrades. Facts have proved that it was extremely
harmful to try to solve ideological issues with administrative measures and mass struggles. The anti-rightist struggle of 1957 was
especially serious in confusing the two kinds of contradictions.
Many comrades were unjustly attacked, while correct views and
good works were wrongly criticized. A large number of writers
and artists were made to suffer, including some of the more talented, promising ones, who had the courage to probe for truths.
This caused a setback in the lively situation resulting from the
policy of "letting a hundred flowers bloom and a hundred schools
of thought contend." In 1958 a tendency to boast and exaggerate
[about economic targets and achievements — Tr.] and to practice
"communism" in the economy swept the nation. Among the intelli-
gentsia a movement was launched to "uproot the white flag" [criticize and repudiate bourgeois ideology — Tr.]. The literary and
art circles also came under these influences and for a while the
"leftist" tendency again surfaced. Literary and artistic issues were
treated in an oversimplified, even vulgarized, manner. Theories
and creative works tended to follow formulas and deal in jargon.
Criticisms became harsh and arbitrary; democracy in the arts
was severely curtailed. This was a profound lesson, one we
must not forget.

What, then, are the main experiences and lessons we must bear
in mind? Briefly, we need to correctly handle three sets of relationships — first, the relationship between the arts and politics, including the question of how the Party should exercise leadership
over work in the arts; second, the relationship between the arts and
the life of the people, or, in terms of artistic practice, the question
of realism in creative works; third, the relationship between inheriting tradition and making innovation — in other words, the question

of how to implement the policy of weeding through the old to develop the new, of making the past serve the present and foreign things serve China. The correct resolution of these three sets of relationships is directly related to the success or failure of socialist literature and art.

Of the three sets of relationships, the most fundamental and decisive is the one between the arts and the life of the people. Literature and art are reflections of social life ... and in turn exert a tremendous influence on life. At all times writers should place themselves in the thick of life, be faithful to life, and write what they are familiar with, what they are interested in, what they react to most deeply, and what they have given a great deal of thought to. Rather than basing their writings on policies formulated for given periods, they should observe, portray, and evaluate life against a broad historical background. It is in this sense that we speak of the unity of the truthfulness and political nature of literature and art. We have been correct in advocating revolutionary realism and revolutionary romanticism, in calling for the portrayal of the heroic people of our time, and in recognizing the guiding role of a correct outlook on life in literary and artistic creation. Such issues as "writing about reality," "the path of realism," and portraying heroic characters and "middle characters" are all academic questions that can be freely discussed. It was wrong to sweepingly label "writing about reality" and "depicting middle characters" as bourgeois or revisionist thinking and denounce them. It was wrong to criticize the 1962 Dalien [Dairen] meeting and the idea of writing about "middle characters." Reality is the lifeblood of art. Without reality a creative work can have no ideological or artistic value....

Comrade Mao Zedong's idea of combining revolutionary realism with revolutionary romanticism in literary and artistic creation has served as a guide in helping writers observe and depict life with accuracy and foresight. Both revolutionary realism and revolutionary romanticism, however, should be rooted in real life. Revolutionary realism often contains factors of revolutionary romanticism, especially when it reflects the future development of reality and the ideals of life. Revolutionary romanticism should be built on realism. Even novels of fantasy cannot be divorced from real life.

Of course no slogan for creative work should be turned into a formula or dogma that fetters creative energy. A writer or artist, as long as he accepts the premise that literature and art must cor-

rectly mirror real life, is free to choose his own method of creation. While we will promote what we believe is the best method of
creation, we should at the same time encourage diverse creative
methods and styles. We should not demand uniformity. The development of literature and art shows that it is both inadvisable and
impossible to make all writers and artists use the same method
of creation. It will only inhibit writers and artists seeking to develop their individual creative talent and impede the flourishing of
creative works.

Writers and artists should make an effort to understand and depict life with the Marxist scientific outlook of life as their guide.
This outlook acknowledges that social life is fraught with contradictions; without contradictions there is no world. Socialist literature and art should have the courage to expose and reflect the contradictions and struggles in life. To face up to contradictions and
expose them or to evade contradictions and cover them up—these
are reflections of two different attitudes toward life and the arts.
Eulogizing and exposing are not incompatible. Rather, they are the
two sides of a question. The important thing here is what stand a
writer or artist takes, what he eulogizes and what he exposes. Literary and artistic works should both portray the bright side of people's life and expose the dark side of society.... Socialist literature and art have the task of both criticism and self-criticism....
We should not only repudiate our enemies but should also take a
critical attitude toward ourselves and our endeavors; otherwise we
cannot make progress. Socialist writers and artists should observe
life, its contradictions and its development, with a clear mind and
sharp insight, be quick to reflect new situations and new problems,
be good at discovering newborn things and progressive forces, and
also have the courage to expose anything that stands in the way of
progress.

The relationship between the arts and politics is in essence one
between the arts and the people. Our literature and art should reflect the life of the people, their needs and interests, in the different periods of the revolution. What we mean by politics is politics
of the classes, politics of the masses, not that of a few politicians,
still less that of a handful of careerists and conspirators. The Party has always formulated its political line and policies in the people's interests, both long term and immediate. Therefore literature
and art, when portraying people's life, cannot be dissociated from
politics, but should be closely linked with politics. As long as lit-

erature and art truthfully reflect the people's needs and interests, they will have a great influence on politics. To insist that literature and art be divorced from politics can only lead them down a wrong path.

In any form of class struggle, political, economic, or theoretical, politics always plays a leading role. But no politician, including a proletarian politician, can guarantee that he will be correct all the time. He cannot avoid making mistakes sometimes. Political lines and specific policies must adapt to changing situations at home and abroad and must be amended and revised as practice demands. Things regarded as correct at one time and place may very well become incorrect at another time and place. Therefore, literature and art, when describing real life, should be suited to the political needs of a given historical period. At the present time they should harmonize with the needs of socialist modernization. Whatever is good for the modernization effort, whatever directly and indirectly inspires people to dedicate themselves to building socialism in China, ... is in the interests of the proletariat and the broad masses of the people. We should not interpret the relationship between the arts and politics in a narrow sense, holding that literary and art works should serve some specific policy or some specific political task of a certain place or time. Politics is not a substitute for the arts. It is not equivalent to the arts. Works that are mere illustrations of policies, that preach or editorialize, that formularize and generalize or are full of slogans will not be accepted by the people because they do not portray the realities of life and lack artistic power.

The aim of our literature and art is to help nurture a new generation of socialist-minded people, elevate the people's spiritual life, help improve and develop socialist society, and meet the people's growing need for cultural life. That is the political task of socialist literature and art. It is wrong to regard literature and art merely as instruments of class struggle and to oversimplify the relationship between the arts and politics. Literature and art can influence politics only through the creation of typical artistic images and through diversified artistic means. The more highly typical the works are, the more varied their artistic means, and the more powerful their ability to move people, the more strongly they can influence politics. ...

The relationship between politics and the arts includes the very important question of how the Party is to lead the work of literature and art. Correct leadership should be the kind that follows a mass line—relying on the masses and including respect for the experts. It should be the kind that tries hard to change itself from nonexpert to expert and to do things according to artistic law. It should not be a patriarchal kind of leadership that issues orders on a personal whim. A writer should be free to write what he wants and in any way he wants. The leadership should not interfere but should be good at giving guidance. The leadership should encourage discussions and debates between differing opinions, allow mistakes and the rectification of mistakes, allow criticism and counter-criticism.

The literature and art of today have evolved from the literature and art of the past. They have a historical continuity and certain national characteristics. However, socialist literature and art are of a brand-new type unlike those of any past epoch. So here we have a question of the relationship between inheriting tradition and making innovation. In his 1956 talk to musicians, which was made public not long ago, Comrade Mao Zedong gave a profound exposition on the correct approach to the Chinese and foreign heritages, on how to preserve national characteristics, and on how to create new works that are socialist and proletarian. We must properly handle the relationship between inheriting tradition and making innovation. Having criticized the conservative tendency, we must guard against the tendency to reject everything national. Having criticized the tendency to be harsh and arbitrary, we must guard against a recurrence of the conservative tendency.

Many traditional operas are now being restaged and are well received by the public. But there are also people who are worried by the reappearance of "emperors, kings, generals, ministers, scholars, and beauties" on the stage. We must make concrete analyses of the plays. Some emperors, kings, generals, and ministers were outstanding contributors to the security and unity of the country or had rendered beneficial services to the people. Some scholars and beauties were rebels who dared to challenge feudal codes of conduct and fight for personal freedom and happiness. We need not only positive characters on the stage but also negative characters people can condemn. We should not drive them all off the stage indiscriminately but should reappraise them from a historical materialist viewpoint and allow them a certain place on the opera stage.

Operatic art should be innovated and developed continuously, in both content and form. It will lose its vitality if allowed to stand still and reject change. Our traditional operas have repertoires of long standing, with well-established methods of artistic expression and highly polished performing techniques. These operas impart historical knowledge and teach people how to tell good from bad, right from wrong, beauty from ugliness. They captivate their audiences with a vigorous national spirit and a great sense of beauty. But under the longtime influence of feudal ideology, the historical events in many operas have been presented in an oversimplified or even distorted way so that the concepts of right and wrong and the moral standards they express are not always correct. These operas also tended to ingrain theatergoers with fixed habits of appreciation. Reforming traditional operas is therefore an arduous task. The reforms should be made energetically but cautiously, boldly but not rashly. We are against both conservatism and unbridled haste. Whatever reforms we make, we should be careful not to damage the national characteristics and artistic essence of the operas; we should improve them, raise them to a higher level, and enrich their powers of expression.

In addition to reforming the traditional operas, we must also create new historical operas from a historical materialist viewpoint. We should use the traditional operatic forms to portray contemporary people and life.... This is necessary if art is to develop. We must not be content with the old national forms but must work hard to develop and create new national forms. We should, on the one hand, weed through the old to develop the new and make the past serve the present, and, on the other hand, adopt all foreign things that are good, remold them, and make them serve China. We should value the achievements of the revolutionary operas on contemporary themes. We should not dismiss them out of hand simply because the Gang of Four tried to take all the credit for the productions, overestimated their success, and called them "model theatrical works."...

TASKS IN THE NEW PERIOD

. . . .

While writers and artists have made bold progress in the last three years.... the works produced so far still fall short of needs....

The process of socialist modernization is a process of great transformation of the productive forces, a profound transformation of both the economy and ideology. This calls for a great emancipation of people's thought.... Since our literature and art have the task of reflecting and promoting this emancipation movement, we writers and artists must first of all emancipate our own minds.... We must break free from the ultra-left trend of thought of Lin Biao and the Gang of Four, from the modern cultism they cultivated, from the influence of feudal and capitalist ideas, from the influence of the widely prevalent narrow-mindedness and force of habit of the small producer, from the influence of dogmatism in literature and art, and from the influence of idealistic and metaphysical concepts of all descriptions....

There is still a resistance to the emancipation of thought in literary and art circles. Some comrades charge that the emancipation of thought in these circles has gone "too far" and has created "confusion" in the people's minds. They blame literature and art for certain wrong ideas that have appeared in society. The charge is unjust. Certainly we must criticize and oppose all wrong ideas, anarchistic tendencies, extreme individualism, and bourgeois "liberalization." But the question now is not that we have gone too far in emancipating thought but that we have not gone far enough. There is still strong resistance and a lot of people's thinking is still ossified or semi-ossified. We can only promote, not hold in check, the emancipation of thought. We can only give correct guidance to, not suppress, the emancipation of thought. Leaders in literary and art circles should begin by emancipating their thought before asking the writers and artists to do so.

To eliminate thoroughly the baleful influence of the ultra-left line, writers and artists are now continuing to hold discussions on the criterion of truth and the criticism of the Summary of the Forum on Literary and Art Work in the Armed Forces. These discussions and criticisms are very important for correcting misconceptions and implementing the Party's principles and policies on literature and art....

Firm implementation of the principle of "letting a hundred flowers bloom and a hundred schools of thought contend" is absolutely necessary if writers and artists are to emancipate their thought.... For years this principle was not properly carried out because of the numerous ideological and political struggles carried out on much wider scales than necessary. Lin Biao and the Gang of Four destroyed the principle altogether. The result: tremendous setbacks in the development of literature and art. It is a profound lesson.

The "Double Hundred" principle has now been written into our

Constitution. This guarantees the people freedom of scientific research and artistic creation. That is to say, we will develop socialist culture and art through the mass line, free competition, and
free debate. We should have faith in the ideological power of Marxism, in the people's creativity and ability to tell good from bad.
We should create an atmosphere most suitable for the free development of science and the arts, for people to write what they want,
speak what they like, and develop their talents fully in order to
bring the initiative and creativity of our writers and artists into
full play....

To achieve this goal, what are the main tasks of writers and
artists?

First, we should energetically promote all kinds of creative work
and help raise our ideological and artistic levels.... We should
encourage writers and artists to go into the thick of life, the richest
source of material for their work, to depict the arduous course of
socialist modernization, to pose and answer the new questions about
which the people are so deeply concerned, and to portray characters
who stand at the forefront of our times and reflect the magnificent
prospect of the new Long March. The writer's main task is to depict the life and destiny of different kinds of people, their complex
personalities and rich spiritual world, and the profound changes in
their mental attitudes as they work for modernization. Our literature and art should depict heroic people, but should also depict other
kinds of people, including average people, backward people, and undesirable people. The works should expose even more forcefully
and profoundly conspirators and careerists like Lin Biao and the
Gang of Four and their followers. They should, in the spirit of
criticism and self-criticism, expose and criticize bureaucratic
habits, the concept of feudal special privileges, the narrow-mindedness and conservatism of the small producer, all old ideas and habits that keep the people in a rut, and bourgeois, petty bourgeois,
and anarchistic ideas that hold back social progress....

Our works should also portray the heroic deeds of the older-
generation proletarian revolutionaries and the martyrs, and restore
the true face of history, which has been distorted by Lin Biao and
the Gang of Four....

When dealing with revolutionary history, we should portray typical proletarian revolutionaries from the historical materialist
viewpoint.... We must be faithful to historical environment and
the real character of historical figures.... The creative works

should correctly express the relationship between the leader and
the masses. While describing the outstanding role of a leader, they
should also show that the masses are the motive force in making
history. Leaders are both the people's guides and public servants
who wholeheartedly serve the people. They are decidedly not omni-
scient and almighty saviors set above the masses. To make a god
of a leader and portray him as one who bestows blessings on the
masses does not fit with the realities of life and the principles of
historical materialism. It distorts the role of leaders and shows
contempt for the people.

Next,...we must also encourage writers and artists to treat other kinds of historical and contemporary themes and to use various
forms and styles in portraying characters of all kinds. This will
help acquaint people with all modes of life and all forms of struggle,
ancient and contemporary, Chinese and foreign, so as to broaden
their vision and enhance their militancy and wisdom....

Third, we should actively promote cultural activities for the
masses in order to further popularize socialist literature and art.
China has a population of more than 900 million, and 800 million of
them live in the countryside. By mass culture we mean mainly socialist culture for the rural areas. If we neglect to educate and en-
lighten the peasants with a new socialist culture, they will remain
fettered by feudal superstition, ignorance, and the backward habits
of the small producer. Their minds cannot be emancipated, and
talk about raising the scientific and cultural level of the entire Chinese nation will, for the most part, become empty words.

On the one hand, we should bring professional performances,
films, books, and periodicals to the countryside, factories, and
mines and the armed forces.... On the other hand, we should encourage amateur cultural activities in factories, mines, the countryside, the armed forces, and city neighborhoods as a means of
discovering new talents....

Fourth, the national minorities inhabit about 60 percent of the
land of China. They have lived and worked for generations on this
vast land, developed their own cultural and historical traditions,
and made great contributions to the development of Chinese culture.
We should continue to help fraternal nationalities develop their culture and art and strengthen the cultural exchange among them.
Since the founding of the new China, we have collected and collated
much of the minority people's traditional literature and art. New
works have appeared one after another.... Our future tasks are

to collect and collate more of the fine oral works of the minority peoples..., revive and improve cultural activities that are a part of local customs as long as they enrich the minority peoples' cultural life, rebuild and expand performing arts groups and research institutions, and train literary and artistic talents, paying special attention to developing the minority peoples' special characteristics.... The exchange among the minority peoples' cultures should result in the enrichment of each people's own culture and art and not the replacement of the culture and art of one nationality by another....

Fifth, we should strengthen Marxist theory and criticism in the field of literature and art....

Mao Zedong Thought, including his thought on literature and art, has always been and still is the guide for our work. Lin Biao and the Gang of Four, in trying to usurp Party power, distorted and trampled on Comrade Mao Zedong's thought on literature and art. They paid no attention to the universal truth and fundamental principles he stated but selected phrases out of context and made some of his statements that were applicable only to a given situation into absolute truths, using them either to deceive or to attack people. This can no longer be tolerated....

We must not regard Marxism-Leninism–Mao Zedong Thought as unchangeable dogma but as a guide to action. We face many new circumstances and new problems unknown to the writers of Marxist classics, Comrade Mao Zedong included. We cannot expect to find in the writings of the revolutionary teachers ready and complete answers to all the problems in our current work. We should restudy Comrade Mao Zedong's works in connection with our own experience and present reality and then investigate, probe, and solve new problems in the new situation.

Instead of merely following the fundamental principles, we should apply and develop them. We should have the courage to revise and supplement those of his directives and statements that do not suit or do not entirely suit the actual situation. We should make our own contributions to enriching and developing Marxist and Mao Zedong's theories on literature and art.

Marxist theories on literature and art originated in foreign countries but must be developed on our own national basis. We should integrate Marxist theory with the practice of the literary and art movement in China and with our long cultural tradition....

Sixth,... we should strengthen and expand cultural exchanges with other countries and develop friendly contacts with writers and artists all over the world. We should utilize all of mankind's fine achievements to enrich our people's cultural life and build up our socialist culture. At the same time we should introduce our socialist culture and our fine traditional arts to the people of the world....

We should learn the strong points and good things of all nations, as Comrade Mao Zedong taught us. But "we must learn with an analytical and critical eye, not blindly, and we must avoid copying things indiscriminately and transplanting mechanically." "We must not adopt their shortcomings and weak points."

It would clearly be dangerous for us if we overlooked the danger of our people and youth's being corrupted by capitalist culture, ideas, and ways of life,...or if we did not strengthen our people's ability to recognize and resist corruption but allowed them to surrender completely to Western capitalist culture and ideas to the extent of losing our national self-confidence and self-respect. We must remain vigilant. We should neither feel overly self-important nor underestimate our own abilities.

THE DUTIES OF THE CHINESE FEDERATION
OF LITERARY AND ART CIRCLES
AND ITS AFFILIATED ASSOCIATIONS

To carry out the glorious missions mentioned above and meet the needs of the new situation, the Chinese Federation of Literary and Art Circles, its local branches and affiliate associations, should be restored. All should earnestly strive to improve their work....
The primary task now is to do everything possible to unite with all writers and artists (including patriotic writers and artists in Taiwan, Hong Kong, and Macao) who can be united, encourage them to expand their talents and knowledge, promote creative, critical, and theoretical work in literature and art, and urge them to wholeheartedly struggle to achieve the Four Modernizations.

The Chinese Federation of Literary and Art Circles is a federated organization of the various literary and art associations. The associations are professional groups of writers and artists (including writers, performers, critics, researchers, translators, editors, teachers of the arts, and organizers of cultural groups) who voluntarily get together to study and practice the arts and promote artistic creation, theory and criticism, and international cultural exchange.

The associations should pay special attention to appointing young and middle-aged writers and artists to leading posts. Their work should be guided by democratic principles and truly demonstrate the nature of people's organizations. . . .

The production of literature and art is creative mental labor done by individuals in conjunction with the collective. The standing organs of the associations should pay full attention to the special characteristics of artistic and literary production. . . . They should encourage diverse subjects, forms, and styles, free competition of different artistic schools, and free discussions of differing literary and artistic views. . . .

First, the associations should take measures to provide the necessary means for professional and amateur writers and artists of all ages to engage in creative work, do research, study, and learn more about life. . . .

Second, the associations should actively help writers and artists study Marxism-Leninism–Mao Zedong Thought in light of reality, study Chinese and world literature and art, and summarize the experience of revolutionary literary and art movements. . . .

Third, the associations should do their very best in cooperation with cultural administrative departments to train more writers and artists to fill the pressing need for trained talent to carry on our work. . . .

Fourth, the associations should assist the Ministry of Education, the Ministry of Culture, and the Central Committee of the Communist Youth League in providing better esthetic education for primary and secondary school students, educating the young people in the appreciation of the arts, and enriching their spiritual life. . . .

Fifth, the associations should protect the creative labor of writers and artists, safeguard all rights, and ensure full freedom of creation, performance, and academic study. The associations have the duty and the right to defend writers and artists against attacks and suppression of their fruits of labor and against illegal acts to deprive them of their right to work, if necessary by appealing and prosecuting cases that come to light.

The associations should look after the welfare of writers and artists and, in cooperation with cultural and publishing departments, establish or revise provisions for remuneration and royalties for works and performances according to the socialist principle "from each according to his ability to each according to his work" and within the limits of present-day economic resources. Awards should be established and award activities revived....

Sixth, the associations should more actively plan and promote international cultural and artistic exchanges....

Comrades:

. . . .

We cannot create a great culture and pioneer a new period of socialist literature and art without daring trailblazers. China needs not just scores of trailblazers but tens of thousands of them.... We are confident that there will be tens of thousands of these literary and artistic pioneers to usher in a new flowering of socialist literature and art....

Translated by Betty Ting
(Wenyibao, 1979, Nos. 11–12)

4

EMANCIPATE THOUGHT
AND ENCOURAGE
LITERARY AND ARTISTIC
DEMOCRACY

Mao Dun

This is an informal speech; my only hope is that it will not make you drowsy.

I

Since the smashing of the Gang of Four, there has been an abundant harvest of short stories and novelettes, which during the past three years have undergone a gradually deepening process and have consequently continued to proliferate.

During the initial period after the smashing of the Gang of Four, although the majority of writings had not divested themselves of "cliquishness," yet there were already some good works worthy of note, such as "The People's Singer," "Sunflower," and others.

"The Class Counsellor" was a major breakthrough. It began to raise questions of concern to the multitude. Other good works of this period include "The Window" and "Self-Sacrifice."

"The Wounded" and "A Mission of Spirit" elicited a wide response; the doings of the Gang of Four were further exposed, and the critical discussion that ensued on all sides was a good phenomenon. When a work gives rise to a diversity of debate, this is an indication of the ideological depth and complexity of its major theme. "The Wounded" and other such works have been called "literature of the wounded" and "exposé literature," which is inappropriate. We need works of this type, for they can — indeed must — cause people of this and the next generation to heighten their awareness and not permit the nightmarish ten years of outrageous behavior of the Gang of Four to recur in China.

The recently published "A Story Badly Edited" and "Black Flag" have criticized the residual influence of ultra-leftist ideology, which cannot be regarded lightly, and have searched for even deeper historical lessons.

The short story "Manager Qiao Assumes Office" describes the
vicissitudes of the struggle to achieve the Four Modernizations.
It symbolizes the multiplicity of themes and is a literary work that
reflects the initial period of the Party Central Committee's epochal
appeal for shifting the emphasis of work.

Novelettes have enjoyed a preliminary flourishing. There are a
certain number of good works known to all: for instance, The
Bloodstained Magnolia, Forever Spring, and others.

I myself feel thusly: in recent years there have been too few
short stories of fewer than ten thousand characters; some novelettes seem to be compressed novels. Moreover, few of these works
are true and penetrating reflections of the spirit of the times. But
this is not a new problem; this phenomenon existed ten or even
twenty years ago. Why? Probably it was caused by the fact that,
even though the authors possessed an abundance of life experience,
they were still not good at grasping the essential elements of their
life experience and eliminating the nonessentials; in other words,
they were not proficient at reshaping their materials. And why was
this so? Probably it was so because the concept of reshaping materials was not yet complete in the authors' minds; that is, either
the authors' knowledge of dialectical materialism and historical
materialism was not yet thorough enough, or they had studied these
things only dogmatically without having truly incorporated them.
We oppose the degeneration of literature to the status of a representation of political slogans, but if we are to arrive at the essential qualities of the complexities and intricacies of real life, to
fathom its mainstream and direction of development, then I fear
that we must arm our brains with dialectical materialism and historical materialism; we must adhere to practice as the sole standard of experiential truth.

Dialectical materialism and historical materialism constitute the
proletarian world view from which we cannot deviate in doing any
task, for if we deviate from this world view, then we will make
mistakes. And for those involved in literature and the arts, this
world view plays a decisive role, because writers and artists are
called "engineers of the human soul," and if they do not possess a
hardened proletarian world view, the works designed and created
by these engineers not only will be poor in quality and unpleasing
in appearance but will be unable to stand the test of time. They
will also give rise in society to results deleterious to the socialist
revolution and socialist construction.

For the past thirty years, our ranks of literary and artistic workers have undergone a fundamental change in comparison with the early post-Liberation period. Now our literary and artistic workers are mainly the new generation of intellectuals nurtured by our Party following Liberation; they are an inseparable part of the working class. Even the older generation of literary and artistic workers from the old society has for the most part been forged and reformed through the education of the Party and long revolutionary experience into working-class intellectuals. However, it cannot be said that our world view has been completely proletarianized and that we need pay no more heed to the question of reforming our world view. Even those literary and artistic workers who come from the working class cannot be said to have been born with a proletarian world view; the theory of so-called "natural redness" is unscientific. Grasping the proletarian world view is a long process, a continuing and never-ending process; it is necessary in the course of diligently, completely, and accurately studying Marxism-Leninism–Mao Zedong Thought to undergo repeated practice and experience before the proletarian world view can be gradually and truly grasped. Once you stop studying Marxism-Leninism and lose faith in practical experience, then you will gradually succumb to ideological rigor and your brain will be addled; your proletarian world view will also gradually deteriorate and you will no longer be able to truly apply this weapon of literature and art to serve the masses of people and the Four Modernizations. Thus our grasp of the Marxist world view is not validated by having read a few classics on historical materialism and dialectical materialism, nor is it satisfied by having some life experience; it is, rather, the work of a lifetime, a lifetime of unceasing work, study, and reform.

II

Of primary importance is the emancipation of thought; this goes for writers as well as for leaders.

Themes must be varied and free of all restrictions; characters must also be varied, and there must be protagonists, antagonists, middle characters, and backward elements — all of these may be written about without restriction. This is something that everyone openly acknowledges. However, there should be a multiplicity of creative styles, and writers should have the freedom to adopt any style they choose.

Originally, the so-called creative style referred to such appella-
tions as realism, romanticism, and critical realism, which are bestowed upon a particular school by the literary theorists after they
have studied its works; it is not the case that the appellation is first
conceived of and then the writers write something to fit that mold.
From his life experiences a writer has feelings, strong feelings,
and when he attempts to express his thoughts using a series of
images, the result is his work. Of course, this author, or any
author, cannot help being influenced by his class background, by the
times, and by his own experiences in observing and participating in
social life. This is why writers of the same era will produce works
that reflect life differently, or even why a single writer's early and
later works will differ in color and basic tone; this is closely related to his personal success or failure, his nearness to or remote-
ness from the people.

The theoreticians study the literary works of the various schools
and propose various categories of styles as well as their features,
defining them in precise terms. Then these styles act reflexively
upon literary workers, becoming the guiding ideology for their
creative work. This is a fact of the history of literature.

The term "socialist realism" was proposed by Stalin, who sum-
marized works as early as Gorky's Mother and as recent as the
works of the early Soviet period, such as Destruction and Iron Flow.
The society of socialist realism is the new society, a society that
has never existed in history, one without exploitation and one which
has a proletarian dictatorship; if this socialist reality is to be expressed, then it is necessary to have a new style. However, although the proposal of this style promoted the development and
proliferation of Soviet socialist literature, authors were not prohibited from continuing to employ the styles to which they had become accustomed; it was only necessary that their works truly reflect some aspect of real life — for instance, what were then known
as the works of fellow travelers. Socialist realism demands that
authors understand the inherent nature of reality from the revolutionary development of reality. The revolutionary development of
reality includes an ideological factor, namely, the ideology of the
communist society, which is the higher stage of socialism. Therefore, the style of socialist realism is, in essence, revolutionary
realism and revolutionary romanticism; the only thing is that this
has never been clearly pointed out.

Chairman Mao proposed a style consisting of a combination of revolutionary realism and revolutionary romanticism after the Soviets had abandoned the slogan of socialist realism (during the Khrushchev era), and he correctly proposed the important factor of revolutionary romanticism. Chairman Mao did not provide a precise definition of this new style; he left that for the theoreticians to determine. And the theoreticians have had to wait for the authors' praxis.

Perhaps some may feel that the praxis of the Soviet writers and the conclusions of the Soviet theoreticians from the time of Stalin's proposing of the style of socialist realism to Khrushchev's emasculation of the revolutionary spirit of this style might serve as an example to us. Of course they may. However, since China's literary tradition differs from that of the Soviet Union, and because our present stage of social development differs from the stage of development of Soviet society under Stalin, the praxis of our authors at this particular time and place must therefore bear the mark of our country's literary tradition and stage of social development. Our theoreticians need only base their summarizing on the works of Chinese authors to derive a concrete and precise definition of the "dual synthesis."

There is such a precedent in the history of world literature. Although the romanticist works of various European countries are similar in fundamental spirit, each bears the brand of its own country's cultural tradition and stage of social development.

As for the question of how the "dual synthesis" style is to be applied to the novel, drama, poetry, and other areas, this is to be determined by the novelists, dramatists, and poets themselves. In this regard, a number of authors have been diligent in their endeavors; however, they have not yet produced completely successful works, and thus the theoreticians are still unable to summarize experience or provide a precise, concrete explanation of the "dual synthesis" style.

My own opinion is that "brave words" cannot be considered as constituting revolutionary romanticism in the "dual synthesis," nor can "futuristic speculation" be considered as constituting revolutionary romanticism in the "dual synthesis." Through the "dual synthesis" style, most authors have sought to mold exemplary heroic characters who advance bravely, revolutionary optimists who are unafraid of hardship and who are ever mindful of the long-range prospects of communism. However, such characters may also be found in revolutionary realist works. Therefore, works employing the "dual synthesis" style should definitely have another nonhypothetical domain above and beyond the molding of such heroic figures, and this can be sought only through a "hundred flowers" liberalization. Only when the writers have written more and better works will the literary theorists and the philosophers be able to give a complete answer. At present, it is important that the theoreticians and philosophers adopt an approach of open and unrestricted debate in dealing with this question, and it is even more important that the writers make use of the "dual synthesis" style to realize in their works the "blooming of a hundred flowers."

At the same time, it is also important to allow writers the freedom to choose their own styles. We cannot make the "dual synthesis" style the method that must be followed, for practice is the sole criterion for determining truth, and practice will tell which of the styles comes the closest to truth. The death of regulation can only be harmful to the blooming of a hundred flowers in the garden of literature and the arts.

Letting a hundred flowers bloom and a hundred schools of thought contend is literary and artistic democracy; some persons are not opposed to letting a hundred flowers bloom and a hundred schools of thought contend, yet they do not approve of literary and artistic democracy. From this we can only infer that their approval of the "Double Hundred" policy is not genuine, or that they want the "Double Hundred" policy to be subject to certain limitations. I think that our slogan should be the blooming of a hundred flowers and the contending of a hundred schools of thought in an environment of literary and artistic democracy. For empty talk of the "Double Hundred" without literary and artistic democracy is contrary to our goal.

III

We have been speaking of carrying on China's literary tradition and emulating foreign countries for many years now. In order to achieve their criminal goal of infiltrating the Party and seizing power, the Gang of Four groundlessly proposed the struggle against Confucianism and Legalism, as though for the past several thousand years of Chinese history there had been no class struggle between the laboring people and the feudal landlords, but only a Confucianist-Legalist struggle; this was nakedly anti-Marxist. Of the pre-Qin philosophers, Han Feizi was a Legalist, and the Han Feizi has been preserved until the present without hiatus; there is little dispute over whether its various chapters were the work of Han Feizi himself. In comparing the teachings of Han Feizi with those of many later politicians, scholars, and literati labeled as Legalists by the Gang of Four, it is quite manifest that the Gang of Four has ridden roughshod over the facts; this is a colossal joke. During the era of the Gang of Four it was impossible to talk of carrying on traditions.

Now, in talking about carrying on traditions, we should cover the entire range from the Classic of Poetry and the Songs of Chu to Zhang Taiyan and Liu Yazi; I regard Liu Yazi as the most outstanding revolutionary poet in the classical style from the last years of the former Qing dynasty until after Liberation. The work Selected Verse of Liu Yazi was published in 1959; Guo Moruo wrote a preface, in which he said that he had written a commemorative verse to the honorable Master Yazi (then in Guilin) on the occasion of his fifty-seventh birthday in 1943, and that Liu Yazi had written a composition, "Imitative Rhymed Response to Moruo on June 8"; Guo included in his preface the text of the verse that he had presented to Liu Yazi, saying,

Compare my verse with the following rhyme of Master Yazi. As poems, the one is but a pale shadow of the other; in terms of emotiveness, Master Yazi is much more positive in expression than I. His final quatrain,

Believe that poor beginnings yield excellence:
   Northward the building seems of consequence.
We'll meet another day at Yuntai;
   You're the stellar void, my house is high.

constituted a scientific prophesy which came true six years later.[1]

In his preface, Guo also compared Liu Yazi to Qu Yuan.[2] Guo Moruo's anthology Of Heaven and Earth contains the piece "A Modern Qu Yuan," the reference being to Liu Yazi. Chairman Mao also held Liu Yazi's poetry in high regard, saying that his poems are "most noble, slighting Chen Liang and Lu You; reading them is most stimulating."[3] Chen Liang's style name was Tong Fu; he was a contemporary of Xin Jiaxuan, and in the collected verse of Xin there is a piece written in harmony with Chen, which also praises Chen. Liu Yazi's poetry reflects the history of the era from the final years of the former Qing dynasty to the founding of the new China, the history of the period of the old Democratic Revolution to the Socialist Revolution, and I think that it would be fitting to call it epic poetry.

The carrying on of tradition includes the artistic component of tradition. Let me give an example: the Yu Tai Xin Yong, compiled by Xu Ling (Xiao Mu) of the Southern Chen dynasty, is regarded as a representative general anthology carrying on the tradition of the Classic of Poetry and the Songs of Chu; the verses in this collection may be deemed heirs to the realist tradition of Chinese poetry. After the beginning of this collection, aside from the eight ancient poems there are six ancient songs, the first of which is "The Sun Rises over the Southeast Corner," which tells the story of Luo Fu (surnamed Qin). It begins, "Luo Fu was skilled at sericulture and gathered mulberry leaves at the south corner of the city wall," and then goes on to describe in detail her dress and adornment; but in describing her appearance, the anonymous author of this ancient song employs the following wording:

> When the traveler saw Luo Fu,
>   He put down his burden and stroked his
>   mustache and beard;
> When the youth saw Luo Fu,
>   He removed his hat and donned his white
>   head scarf.
> The plower forgot his plow,
>   The hoer forgot his hoe;
> To and fro they went, scolding and forgiving
>   each other.
> They could only sit there, watching Luo Fu.

This is ten times as effective as a direct description of the appearance of a beautiful woman; there is no mention of Luo Fu's appearance, and yet her magnificent beauty has found its way onto the page. This is truly an unprecedented example of descriptive technique. Most of the forewords or prefaces of the currently reprinted classical poetic works only mention that the work has a certain ethnicity, and there is seldom any mention of technique; this is truly fooling ourselves.

With regard to emulating foreign works, I think that we should read Greek and Roman mythology, Scandinavian mythology, the epic poems of Homer, and the Greek tragedies. In the Iliad, Homer uses "the courage of flies" to describe the audacious bravado of the warriors of the two opposing forces. This usage is great because, when flies see sugar or something else that they like to eat, they head toward it in droves; you can chase them away, but they'll be back in an instant — this is something that all of us see often.

The use of flies as an analogy is very fresh and yet commonplace; it comes from life, yet it is in fact something that others did not think of. This is much better than using tigers, leopards, or lions to describe the courage of warriors, because the courage of these animals is not often seen.

Not only the nineteenth-century European romanticist, realist, and critical realist literature but also medieval chivalric literature, the literature of the European Renaissance, and the classical literature of the eighteenth century all contain exemplary elements.

For writing historical novels, we may learn some techniques from the historical novels of Scott and Dumas, although these two historical novelists depart from historical fact and often engage in empty and subjective fabrication, which is to be eschewed. The historical novel allows for fictional characters and events, but they must be compatible with characters and events of the period; otherwise, it is just so much fabrication.

If, in continuing the Chinese literary tradition and borrowing from foreign literature, we are to read famous works both ancient and modern, Chinese and foreign, we come upon the question of appreciation. If you cannot appreciate a work, then how are you to continue its tradition or borrow from it? A writer's appreciativeness and expressiveness are two sides of the same coin. It is quite difficult to imagine a very expressive writer who does not have a corresponding appreciativeness. In both ancient and modern times and in China as well as abroad, there has probably never been a writer who could produce a superior work but who lacked the ability to discern the superior and inferior aspects of the work of others. In fact, the stronger a writer's expressiveness, the more often he is able to uncover as yet undiscovered superiorities in the work of others and the more often he is able to reveal deficiencies as yet unobserved by others.

Expressiveness is not inborn; it is cultivated by deeply penetrating life, by participating in the fiery struggle, and from the accumulation of life experiences — we might say that it is learned from life itself.

For those young people with literary aspirations, I have a suggestion: before you begin to write, it is best to read the works of others and try to analyze them. You must make a concrete analysis and point out what is good and what is inadequate in their structures, characters, and settings. And do not use such banalities as "I read it and was deeply moved" or "I found it so inspiring" as a substitute for concrete analysis. If this is not possible, then you should read how the critics have analyzed a particular piece. And it is not enough to read only one critique; you must read several, and if there are opposing critiques, you should compare and study them. If you are persistent, then the day will come when you will be able to analyze the works of others, and only then will you be able to attempt to write about a theme with which you are familiar.

IV

The literature of connivance of the Gang of Four nonsensically claimed that only works about the "capitalist-roaders" had "depth" and that only works that wrote more about the "capitalist-roaders" had more "breadth." Such misconceptions regarding the question of the depth and breadth of life must be eliminated.

The work object of workers in literature and the arts is social life; it is the relations between people at all levels of society, their contradictions and struggles, their spiritual state, their thought and consciousness, etc. For this reason, workers in literature and the arts must simultaneously have the sharp ideological weapons of dialectical materialism and historical materialism as well as broad and trenchant life experiences. With regard to life, workers in literature and the arts must be able not only to stand tall and have a wide view of the overall picture but also to penetrate deeply and have an overall and thorough understanding of the actual events about which they write. Standing tall and penetrating deeply is a dialectical relationship. We must be familiar with various aspects of life; we must first understand the overall situation and then deeply penetrate one aspect of it. It is very hard to imagine how someone who has deeply buried himself in one particular aspect (for instance, a workshop in a factory or a production brigade in a village or some other corner of life) and who knows nothing at all about anything else could engage in creative work. Of course, he could write reportorial literature, but if he is going to write about typical characters in typical settings, so that the life reflected in his work possesses universality, then his own little corner of life is no longer enough. That which we express in creative praxis must be a social life that has general significance, but the stories and characters that we fabricate must be stories and characters in a concrete setting. To be able to fabricate stories and characters and to be able to reflect universal social life is not solely a question of writing technique but in fact is also a question of under-standing the whole and of deeply penetrating one aspect of it. Tech-nique comes from life. The ancient song "The Sun Rises over the Southeast Corner" and Homer's analogy of the flies in the Iliad are good examples.

Yet these two examples belong to the portion of literary work dealing with the description of objects and events. The question of technique in works of literature and art includes analyzing, syn-thesizing, and refining the fundamental materials of life as well as defining the conception of the major theme; all of this requires the author's long-term penetration of life and participation in the fiery struggle. And today we must also participate in eliminating the residual poison of the Gang of Four and throw ourselves into the swirling tumult of uplifting the nation and serving the Four Modern-izations. In such a life there will be certain events or persons that will make a deep impression on a writer, stimulating him and mak-ing it hard for him to forget them; then, through the interaction of imagistic and logical thought, the writer's thought structure will mature and he will begin to write.

All of this has to do with the roots of the question of technique — it all comes from life. And the problem of technique should be re-garded from such an elevated vantage point; writing skills should be thus forged. As for the structure of a work and the description of setting and characters, these are questions of technique belonging to the area of skills. Here we may continue to derive inspiration from carrying on the Chinese literary tradition and from looking to foreign literary works, thereby gradually distilling many of our predecessors' virtues and making them our own.

V

Life is the source of literature and art. Now, as our country seeks to realize the Four Modernizations, this source is unprece-dently magnificent, great, unique, and varied: it is the crystalliza-tion of the people's determination, wisdom, and imagination.

The task of those writers and artists able to give expression to such an era is a glorious one, but it is also a difficult one.

In addition to having an overall understanding of life and deeply penetrating one aspect thereof, we must also have an understanding of the history of our own country and of the other countries of the world; we must have an understanding of the torrent of international struggle; and we must also have an understanding of China's and other countries' economic structures. Moreover, in order to make our works serve the Four Modernizations, we cannot be without at least a basic understanding of modern science.

During the Ming dynasty there was a man by the name of Yang Shen (Sheng Yan) who wrote a book called Ballads of the Twenty-One Dynastic Histories. His purpose was to provide a reference from which a basic knowledge of history could be gained. During the early years of the Republic, Cai Dongfan wrote many elaborations of colloquial tales, taking his material from the twenty-four dynastic histories and covering the period from Qin and Han up to Republican China, under the general title of Colloquial Tales from Chinese History. When the portion of this work on the Republic was separately published, forty chapters written by Xu Jinfu were added, the work being called Colloquial Tales from the Republic. This work was reprinted just a few years ago, but it was for internal sale only and was not available to the general reading public. And there is another book, titled An Explanation of Qing History.[4] I hope that these books can be reprinted and openly published.

At the same time, I am suggesting that comrades in the area of folk arts break down the important events of history into sections and write them out, setting them to music. In this way, the broad audiences will be given some historical learning, which will be of inestimable value.

Today's young and middle-aged writers must not only spend more time studying in the areas of continuing Chinese traditions and borrowing from foreign works, but they must also engage in extra study of the history of China and of the other countries of the world. They must also absorb an understanding of international politics, economics, and modern science as mentioned above (older authors also need work in these last three areas). With such a multiplicity of tasks, it seems that one hardly knows where to begin; but there is always a way.

The China Federation of Literary and Art Circles and its branches in the various provinces and municipalities, as well as the various national associations and their provincial and municipal branches, should come to a clear understanding of the situation and, in the spirit of seeking truth from facts, draw up programs based on the foregoing requirements. If we but adhere to literary and artistic democracy and collective concern for the greater welfare, we will be able to draw up such programs. It matters not that there may be a great many slightly different programs; let us try them all and find, through practice, those which are best. This conference marks the beginning of springtime in literature and the arts; the real work is still ahead of us. I am old and weary, and I want to follow your lead in striving to advance. I have said much, and some of it is probably in error; therefore, comrades, I ask for your guidance. Finally, I hope that the format of the group discussions can be modified from the formal, long-winded presentation to the jocular and spirited type where much more is meant than said. Only in this way will we all have a chance to speak and at the same time avoid banality, boasting, and blather. As for those major theses having copious content and incisive interpretations, I am sure that all the journals will be vying for publication rights.

Translated by Philip Robyn
(Renmin wenxue, 1979, No. 11)

NOTES

[1]Quoted from Selected Verse of Liu Yazi, Guo's preface, p. 3.
[2]See Guo's preface, p. 2.
[3]Selected Verse of Liu Yazi, p. 150.
[4]Originally written by Wang Rongbao, emended by Xu Guoying.

5

OPENING ADDRESS TO THE THIRD CONGRESS OF THE CHINESE WRITERS ASSOCIATION

Liu Baiyu

Delegates and Comrades:

The Third Congress of the Chinese Writers Association is now in session.

It has been twenty-six years since the convening of the Second Congress of the Federation of Writers and Artists in the fall of 1953 and nineteen years since the Third Expanded Session of the National Committee of the Chinese Writers Association in the summer of 1960. In the interim, our country experienced a glorious but tortuous period of struggle, and our literary front also endured the grueling trial brought on by the tempest of a struggle. Now our country has entered into a new historical era, which aims at achieving the Four Modernizations. The convocation of this congress occurs at a crucial time when the Party is reordering its priorities and when the people of the entire country, with one heart and mind, are advancing toward the goals of modernization. Indeed, this gathering is of great historic significance, with over six hundred veterans and new recruits from the literary front assembled under one roof to discuss the critical issue of promoting literature to serve the Four Socialist Modernizations.

During the past few days, you have been earnestly studying and discussing the Congratulatory Message presented by Comrade Deng Xiaoping on behalf of the Central Committee and the State Council to the Fourth Congress of Chinese Writers and Artists. It is the general feeling that this message is a vital document providing guidance by the Party on literature and art, summarizing in detail the achievements and basic experiences on the battlefront of literature and art since the founding of the nation, and clearly defining the direction and path for literature and art in a new socialist era. You have also thoroughly discussed Comrade Zhou Yang's report,

entitled "Inherit the Past and Usher In the Future — For a Flourishing Literature and Art in the New Period of Socialism" and delivered on behalf of the China Federation of Literary and Art Circles. The Congress of the Chinese Writers Association is an inte-
gral part of the Fourth Congress of Writers and Artists. In our
congress we must continue to study in earnest Comrade Deng's
Congratulatory Message, discuss in greater depth Comrade Zhou
Yang's report, sum up the basic experiences of the literary movement in the thirty years that followed the founding of the nation,
analyze new situations and problems on the literary front, clarify
the role of literature in a new socialist era, mobilize and arouse
old and new writers of every ethnic group in the country, and, especially, nurture young writers from the new generation, so that
with dedication and enthusiasm we can unite to look to the future
and wage a valiant struggle for the blossoming of socialist literature and art. Such is the policy and theme of the Congress of
Writers and Artists and of our congress as well. Following this
policy and stressing this theme, we should strive to conduct a good
conference that will develop democracy, strengthen unity, and stimulate the creation of literature.

Leading comrades of the Party have requested that we focus our
energies on debating the important issues of the policy and mission
of contemporary literature and art.

How literature can serve the Four Modernizations is an issue
that generates relatively more discussion and requires a clear answer. Socialist modernization is another great revolutionary transformation in our history. Literature must vividly portray and actively promote this historic movement. In order for literature to
serve the Four Modernizations, there must be more and better literary works to satisfy the daily increasing cultural needs of the
masses of a new era and to inspire and stimulate them to engage
in selfless labor and struggle. Socialist literature must scream
and shout, sound the gong, and clear the way for the Four Modernizations. The road for literature to serve the Four Modernizations
is extremely wide, and the ways to serve are many. In upholding
the premise that literature should be for the broadest masses of
people — first and foremost for the workers, peasants, and soldiers — diversity in themes, forms, genres, and styles should be
encouraged. We ardently advocate the depiction of real life under
socialism and the reflection of this great present historic transformation from every angle. However, this is not to imply that only

themes about life under modern socialist construction can serve
the Four Modernizations. Modern and contemporary revolutionary
historic themes, as well as ancient historical themes, can also perform this function, provided they are true to the needs of the time
and the people, helping to boost the people's will to do battle and
their national confidence, enhancing their knowledge of history and
of life, and fostering their idealism. Modern themes are themselves quite diverse. Based completely on what they observe, hear,
feel, and believe, writers can, from different aspects, select different angles to mirror the wonderful and multifaceted life of our age.
To portray the progressive characters in the new Long March and
to fashion the heroic images of our times is the moral obligation
of the writers. At the same time, they should also create from real
life all kinds of characters, such as bureaucrats, opportunists,
careerists, etc. Literature must realistically and vividly mirror
the heroic deeds of the masses in their labors and must also attack
and criticize reactionary forces and negative elements that obstruct
the Four Modernizations, so as to propel unceasingly forward our
life in this great age.

We must achieve a new breakthrough in literature and make a
meaningful contribution to the promotion of literary works. Besides emphatically criticizing the ultra-leftist line and adhering to
the policy of "Letting a hundred flowers bloom and a hundred
schools of thought contend," the most important issue is to encourage and urge writers to actively participate in the noble struggle
for the Four Modernizations and to identify with a new age and a
new people. Be they writers of realistic or historical themes, they
must synchronize their breathing with that of the masses, share in
the same destiny, maintain flesh-and-blood ties with them, and be
involved with their each and every concern. Only then can the
writers adequately express the spirit of our age, voice the aspirations of the masses, and truly become honest spokesmen for the
people.

Comrades, during this congress, we also need to discuss the re-
vision of the Constitution of the Chinese Writers Association and
to elect a new leadership so that it will truly become a people's
organization where the writers themselves take charge. To elect
a leading body with exemplary working style, administrative knowledge, and the ability to fight is the wish of the members and also
the dream of a billion readers. We must not disappoint the country's writers, critics, translators, and literary editors in their

expectations and trust; imbued with a sense of responsibility toward the masses, we must promote democracy to its fullest extent and successfully accomplish this assignment together.

Let us unite more closely and work even harder to create literature, to sound the war drums for the Four Modernizations, and to raise our voices in battle cry, scaling the heights of world literature and struggling for the beginning of a new golden age for socialist literature.

Translated by Ellen Yeung
(<u>Wenyibao</u>, 1979, Nos. 11–12)

6

NO BREAKTHROUGH, NO LITERATURE

Bai Hua

I greatly value this chance to address the Fourth Congress of Chinese Writers and Artists. It has been twenty years since I saw many comrades and comrades-in-arms, and my memories of them seem to belong to a different lifetime. During these past years many comrades and comrades-in-arms have faced imminent death a hundred times with only a single hope of living on. Yet, after all that, they are here to meet with one another, to talk over old times, and to look back at what is past and contemplate what lies ahead. But some comrades and comrades-in-arms have left us forever. We remember that they once hoped and struggled just as we did. They have bequeathed their hopes and struggles to us.

I would like to speak of my feelings on a few points:

MORE AND MORE PEOPLE
WERE AWAKENED

Over the past half century our great people has, under the leadership of the Communist Party, carved out a road to national survival with the riverlike torrent of our crimson blood. We have been awakened from our feudal ignorance. A great people's republic was established precisely because more and more people were awakened, because the ranks of fighters were swelled and our victories multiplied. What a glorious morning our nation had! In that morning we were wide awake, and we made great sacrifices in pursuit of our goals. At that time our Party was full of confidence. The Party had limitless strength and everyone responded to its summons, because it had taken root among the people. In those early years, even our bitterest enemies had to admit that the people of China had stood up and were moving forward. No external pressure could push us backward or subvert this nation.

But later we did move backward and were in danger of being subverted. Lin Biao and the Gang of Four carried out their obscurantist policies, using the people's gratitude and reverence toward the Party and its leaders to make increasing numbers of people revert to a state of ignorance. How could this have happened? First, this happened because they took a distorted version of what was really a scientific ideology — Marxism-Leninism — and methodically imposed it as a religious ideology. They did not allow the scientific study and discussion of Marxism-Leninism–Mao Zedong Thought; predictably, this made the correct understanding and development of these ideas impossible. They deified a revolutionary leader by means of authoritarian government and mass movements, and the majority of people did not dare to oppose or doubt them. Even today, when we oppose modern-day superstition and advocate science, we are beset from all sides, just as the men who smashed idols before the 1911 Revolution were surrounded and killed by crowds. The death of Zhang Zhixin* happened this way. The blood of this martyr has awakened increasing numbers of people, but there are still those who cling to their superstitions and others who pretend to be devout believers out of selfish motives. People who cling to delusions are to be pitied, but people who pretend to be believers are to be despised. We have no choice but to use every ounce of strength, like the silkworm, to bite through the cocoon we have made for ourselves. Only then can we get air and sunlight; only then can we have space in which to live and develop.

For a long time we have unstintingly opposed the tendency toward formulism and jargonism in literary works, but we have never succeeded in getting rid of these tendencies. Formulism and jargonism exist because literature played a role in the attempt to remake men into gods. Every writer and artist can remember the time when the image of any Party cadre in his works had to be the personification of the Party, and the image of any worker had to represent the entire working class. Ultimately, "people" disappeared from literature, leaving nothing but a few anemic generalities. Literature too played an important role in spinning the cocoon of ignorance. We Chinese are a good, upright people, and good, upright people are gullible. Right up until the time that Lin Biao and

---

*A woman Party cadre in the area of literature and art who questioned the authority of Jiang Qing. She was arrested, imprisoned, tortured, and executed (in 1975) at the age of forty-five. — H. G.

the Gang of Four practiced "absolute dictatorship" over the masses, we unquestioningly kept in mind the formula that achievement is supreme while shortcomings and mistakes are only part of the whole — one finger out of ten. For a long period many people even believed that the Gang of Four was truly carrying out a revolution. Owing to ignorance, some formerly courageous fighters lost the ability to stand up the enemy, and, had it not been for the negative example provided by this bunch, even more of us would have gone to our deaths unawakened. The outcry raised by a million people on Tomb-Sweeping Day, 1976, was long regarded by certain people as illegal. Without the awakening of increasing numbers of people, the Gang of Four would not have been smashed with one blow on October 1, 1976. Without the awakening of increasing numbers of people, millions of cadres and citizens would not have been liberated. Without the awakening of increasing numbers of people, normal debate could not unfold among people of different viewpoints, including those who label others "back-stabbers." Without the awakening of increasing numbers of people, the present emphasis on realism in creative writing would not have appeared, the Fourth Congress of Chinese Writers and Artists would not have been held, and many old comrades would not be gathered here now. Without the awakening of increasing numbers of people, China's Four Modernizations would have no hope and literature would have no hope!

WHAT ARE YOU TRYING TO DO?

Recently some people have severely condemned trends in creative writing during the three years since the smashing of the Gang of Four. They constantly demand an answer to this question: "What are you trying to do?" This question must be met head-on.

What are we trying to do? We are trying to renew the tradition of realism in our country's literature! We are trying to bring back literature's minimal function — the reflection of life in society. We are trying to make people remember the painful lessons of history. We are trying to help them distinguish good from evil, right from wrong. We are trying to renew the people's faith in socialist revolution. We are trying to help the people be aware of China's present situation, as well as the difficulties and promises that await us on the road ahead. The past three years of practice in creative writing give ample explanation of our aims. What then makes some people still feel that this is strange and incomprehensible? I think that it is only to be expected, since for a long time we have had people pointing at a deer and calling it a horse. Now that the real horse has appeared, people do not recognize it, and they brand the man who calls a horse a horse a heretic.

In this new era, if artists and writers turn aside from the profound social and ideological struggles before us, if they are unwilling to gain an understanding of life and the fresh, lively thought of the masses right now, their works will not be read. Thus it is not merely a problem of what we are trying to do but also of what we should do. Should we cover up social contradictions that no one can possibly cover up? Should we sing the praises of the ignorance that caused our people to suffer great losses? Should we keep silent about the bureaucratism that even now impedes our forward motion? Should we give credence to "one man's rule is law," which has nothing in common with the Party? The people will not allow it. If you insist on going ahead with it, then go do it. You may have the opportunity to publish your work and you may have plenty of paper, but you will have fewer and fewer readers.

The Gang of Four was in power for a period of ten years, longer than the War of Resistance against Japan. Shouldn't we give some thought to why the history of this period was so unusual? Didn't the Third Plenum of the Eleventh Party Congress win the support of an overwhelming majority of people precisely because Party Central renewed its commitment to seek the truth in facts and speak truthfully to the people? The Party is battle headquarters, and the masses are soldiers. If headquarters does not pass on information about the enemy, how can the soldiers destroy the enemy and gain victory?

Our mission as writers and artists is given us by history. All those who go against the laws of historical progress by putting pressure on literature to make it serve their political interests will ultimately fail. Let us not neglect this extraordinary chapter of history. Let us study its origin and development, its bloodcurdling successes, and its tragic, shameful failure. In human history there is no calling so fated to have its glory judged by history as is creative writing. Lin Biao, the Gang of Four, and that "counselor" of theirs once rode roughshod over Chinese writers in a multitude of ways. And didn't some of the Gang of Four's imperial theorists and henchmen see their political careers come to an end, regardless of their importance? In the brief thirty years of new

China's literary history, with all its changes and reverses, there
are many lessons to be learned. Chinese writers have their streak
of hardheadedness. A large number were beaten to the ground by
"leftist" theoretical henchmen, where they were buried in the soil
for over twenty years. But haven't they come back to life? Haven't
they started to sprout and blossom in preparation for bearing fruit?
Seeds are not afraid of soil. Seeds buried in soil are in a perfectly
suitable place. The book Fresh Flowers Abloom Again makes clear
where to place merit and blame for what took place in the literary
world during the last twenty-some years. History will never obliterate Li Bai, Du Fu, or Sima Qian, but it did obliterate powerful
men of Li Bai's, Du Fu's, and Sima Qian's times, prominent though
they were. Many writers who for years could not take up their pens
to write are still alive today. Though the flesh of many comrades
has been destroyed, their works are still in existence today.
Haven't all those henchmen who used to be "golden clubs" turned
into hempen stalks? After thirty years of literary criticism, how
many articles can be published without alteration for people to read
today? Doesn't this explain where the problem lies? Of course
this was brought about by an intricate series of historical factors;
no one is going to start probing around for proof of individual responsibility. But we must be cognizant of twists and turns in the
course of history.

Now Party Central and the people have given writers a basic
right — the right to express one's own point of view. People all
over the country are taking part in the debate on the question of
literature, a question that is intimately tied up with people's lives.
Once the masses have found their voice, we can be sure that the
truth will become increasingly clear through debate. The recent
discussion of "eulogizers" and "back-stabbers" is beneficial to
comrades in the literary world and to people throughout the country
[the "eulogizers" are criticized for singing the praises of the
Party's virtue, while the "back-stabbers" are said to be deficient
in virtue — Tr.]. We cannot carry on the discussion without first
getting a clear idea of "virtue." Even today some comrades cannot
distinguish between the Gang of Four and the Party, between Marxism-Leninism and pseudo-Marxism-Leninism, or between the people's interests and special privileges. They protect the nation-
afflicting, people-crippling cancer of the Gang of Four's extreme left
line as if it were part of the tissue of Marxism-Leninism. They do
not allow people to touch upon this problem: those who do are anti-

Party "back-stabbers." Comrade Zhang Zhixin, who recognized the cancer in our Party's tissues, was thought to be a criminal plotting to murder the revolution and was executed. She was able to meet her death without wavering because of her firm loyalty to and deep love for the Party, for Marxism-Leninism and for the people.

Earlier this year, I spoke this sentence at the National Conference on Poetry: "Fellow poets! Let us never again sing the praises of any 'world savior.' " I reiterate this today because I still feel the same way. The reason is quite simple: "There has never been a 'world savior.' " This line from the International Workers' Song was sung by countless martyrs to our cause as they went to their deaths. Martyrs to our cause have told us that "there has never been a world savior." So why should we sing the praises of something that has never existed? Some true believers who pretend to go to every length in their devotion insist that there is such a thing as a savior in this world. They connect the concepts of savior and revolutionary leader, sometimes even equating the two in order to intimidate others. Now that Comrade Zhang Zhixin has come to life again as a woman and revolutionary in the hearts of increasing numbers of Chinese, it is time to ring down the curtain on the cruel farce of deifying one man in order to kill others!

THE SO-CALLED QUESTION OF "SAFETY"

I often receive letters from well-meaning comrades and readers cautioning: "You are in a dangerous position!" I am grateful for their concern. It is quite reasonable for them to think this way. We Chinese have many excellent qualities, one of which is honesty. At certain times many honest people have lost their jobs, their freedom, their basic necessities, and even their heads. At the same time quite a few nonworking hypocrites rely on intimidating others to gain reputation, profit, and official rank. Of course they are people who upset the boat and fall into the water, like Yao Wenyuan, but when all is said and done these are in the minority. A few years ago, vivid stories of rising to heights of eminence by lying appeared every month, year in and year out, to educate Chinese people, young and old, thus leading to a notion prevalent in our society: Hypocrites are safe, while honest men are in danger. I often hear comrades with children say apprehensively: "My son is bound to go to

prison someday, because he doesn't know how to lie." And some
comrades say with smug satisfaction: "My son is bound to make
something of himself, because at his age he's already a double-
dealer." How sad!

While still a teenager I walked out of a Guomindang-controlled
area rife with agents and undercover detectives to join the army.
In the smoke of battle I felt I was living in a warm home, as safe as
could be. Whether we were marching or in battle I kept a journal
every day to reveal and analyze my thoughts and record everything
I took an interest in. In the late fifties all my writings were turned
into grounds for accusations that I could not explain away. The
most innocent remarks became treacherous anti-Party diatribes.
From then on I never again kept any sort of diary or notebook. It
goes without saying that during the Cultural Revolution the written
word was something to be feared, but the spoken word was especially liable to bring on disaster. It was like walking at the edge of an
abyss or stepping on thin ice. After "Down with everything: all
out civil war" became an accepted slogan, every person was con-
scious of danger. The conversation of normal people was reduced
to guarded whispers. After the Gang of Four was smashed, and
particularly when Party Central convened the Third Plenum of the
Eleventh Party Congress to carry out the great amount of work
needed to sweep away disorder and return to normalcy, fewer and
fewer people have been incriminated by their own words. But we
cannot say that the alarm has been completely revoked. The lesson
that most intellectuals have learned from personal experience is
that when you are permitted to speak your mind there is already a
latent risk that censorship will be tightened. When you speak your
mind you are setting yourself up to be beaten, to be labeled counterrevolutionary, or to be put in prison. The current of anti-Third
Plenum sentiment that appeared this spring makes this clear.

When the story of the circumstances of Comrade Zhang Zhixin's
death came out in the papers, many comrades were filled with
righteous indignation, which strengthened their fighting spirit and
resolve. There were also many who could not help but rub their
necks in secret relief as they thought of how fortunate they were in
having kept their throats intact by keeping their mouths shut. But
just what sort of socialist nation is this where Communist Party
members don't dare speak the truth at Party meetings; where fathers and sons, brothers, sisters, and friends cannot confide in one
another; where writers dare not jot down thoughts in notebooks and

citizens dare not keep diaries? Our people have a strong sense of responsibility, and so do our writers. The source of our courage is none other than this sacred sense of responsibility. The people of this country trust that Party Central will never go back on its promises to them. Comrades in the literary world have weathered such a long and tortuous period of history that their reasoning powers have been strengthened. In academic matters the possibility of doing away with the hundred schools of thought no longer exists. If we choose we can let the doctrines of a given school of thought go in one ear and out the other; we can listen and debate the issues or we can leave the place of discussion. We cannot look to organization and discipline for help in academic matters, unless another Gang of Four comes along and enacts the same fascist policies. But if that day should come, more than a few people will meet with disaster.

It cannot yet be said that this is a fairly safe time for writers. Aren't people still writing essays, sending letters, and making speeches asking to lock up so-and-so or to label so-and-so a counterrevolutionary? Once one takes part in literary work it is imperative to speak one's mind and make a statement about life. Out of this arises the problem of "eulogizers" versus "backstabbers," the problem of personal safety and the problem of offending people. But what is one to do, short of getting out of this line of work altogether? In "Between Men and Ghosts" Comrade Liu Binyan wrote an epigram rebuking cadres who give up their convictions: "They dare not give offense in other respects; only when it comes to the 'masters' of this republic — the people — are they unafraid to offend."

We need to turn this sentence around and see that it is carried out: "We dare to give offense in other respects; only when it comes to the 'masters' of this republic — the people — are we afraid to offend." It goes without saying that we depend upon socialist democracy and legal accountability for our safety, but more importantly we depend upon the masses. Who is in the most dangerous position today? The Gang of Four, that's who. Their days are passed in trembling, and prison has become the safest place for them to live. There are other individuals who are not safe, though they have climbed to the pinnacle of power. They will eventually be thrown out by the people; this is inevitable. Looking at it in this sense, as long as we speak the truth for the sake of our mother — the people — and discharge our obligation to history, we can say with complete assurance that the people will protect us and history will pass equitable judgment upon us.

CARRY OUT THE "DOUBLE HUNDRED" POLICY

The artistic and intellectual liveliness of the past three years holds forth great hope for us. I am confident that if we can keep going in this way, some very good literary works will appear within three to five years. Today all sorts of different opinions can be brought out for debate. Of course some comrades adopt an immoderate tone in their zeal, even to the point of hurling indiscriminate abuse. But none of this can affect the overall outlook of gradual improvement. This situation is unique in our thirty-year history. Having passed through the ten-year calamity caused by Lin Biao and the Gang of Four, given the present state of affairs, we should value and strive to solidify and develop these propitious circumstances.

In the first place, many notable literary works have appeared. In the past three years, old, middle-aged, and young writers have worked industriously and courageously to bring forth a large number of works. The depth and breadth of life touched upon by these works is unprecedented. Our literature is showing signs of coming back to life, and we owe it all to the potion called "realism." The mainstream of literary creation over the past three years has taken a healthy course. The overwhelming majority of writers are filled with earnest devotion for their country and their people. They are outraged by the losses suffered in their time, and they strike boldly at current ills. They extract their crimson hearts and hand them over to their readers. Their hearts and the hearts of the people are as one. Writers have never been as close to the people as they are today. But there is still an atmosphere of tension in our ranks. Bold assertions, clear denials, and sharp, penetrating critical essays are still few and far between. Without debate there can be no clear idea of truth and falsehood. The discussions regarding "eulogizers and back-stabbers" and the story "Manager Qiao Assumes Office" have been excellent.

Once opinions are put in written form, our leaders can also take part in the discussions by writing articles; but they should not prohibit discussion or punish those who take part, nor should they constantly compel people to engage in self-criticism. Permitting the dissemination and advocacy of opposing opinions means that academic discussion must be allowed to unfold on equal terms. Leading comrades should be broad-minded and tolerant; narrow-minded leaders are no good to the Party. Comrade Deng Xiaoping said it so well in the Congratulatory Message he gave on behalf of Party Central: "The magisterial approach must be done away with. The issuing of executive orders in the areas of literary and artistic creation and criticism must be stopped. If we view such things as upholding Party leadership, the result will be the opposite of that intended." But there are those who will not determinedly enforce this policy simply because Party Central told them to, for they are incapable of anything but "peremptory interference." If they could not do this they would be unemployed. "Peremptory interference" is much less troublesome than an exchange of opinion on equal terms. It is as if bringing the wit and intelligence of writers into play would make these people seem lacking in wit and intelligence.

Some people ask: "Why should writers and artists have any special conditions to live and work under? Wouldn't special conditions lead to revisionism?" "How can leaders and followers get equal or nearly equal incomes? Wouldn't that be egalitarianism?" See how difficult it is to implement a political policy! What's more, Party Central only suggested a few correct principles pertaining to leaders with authority over literature. I have never heard of anyone's being dismissed from office, demoted, or given a cut in salary for ultra-leftist persecution of intellectuals, much less going to trial and being punished. Because of this we must carry out a long and tireless struggle before we can win improvements in the basic conditions provided for literary work.

In the past few years many writers have grown old and died without visiting one another. This was not because they did not want to visit, but because they did not dare to. Beginning in 1957, when "secretive personal associations" became grounds for criminal charges, who dared to keep up his "personal associations"? Anti-Party cliques were constantly being ferreted out. Moreover, we were "drifting apart, each in his own way." Many comrades "looked unrecognizingly at one another, like strangers on the road." Throughout history, both in China and abroad, scholars have always had literary friends, academic friends, and fellow connoisseurs of poetry. Try to learn without asking questions, and you'll never make any progress. It has gotten somewhat better the last three years, but comrades whose fears have not yet abated still dare not go to gatherings of intellectuals. As soon as a large group gets together, they get nervous. For a number of years we weren't able to let each other know who was dead and who was alive. Today everyone views what happened to young authors in 1957 as a sobering lesson; the problem is that while some view it as a lesson in what not to do, others are still viewing it in reverse! Even today some people take a jaundiced view of us. My experience has taught me to disregard them, because standards of honor and disgrace have always been set by history and by the people. Our subtropical plants grow in special abundance when they interact competitively to form a natural community. Different types of plants grow together, each [type] with its own niche, each adjusting to the other's presence, each giving shade or protection to the other. Let our old, middle-aged, and young authors also form a natural community!

HOPES AND EXPECTATIONS

I call for democracy! The China Federation of Literary and Art Circles and the Chinese Writers Association are organizations of writers themselves. They are popular associations under the leadership of the Party. I hope they are not disguised bureaus or offices of a certain ministry. If writers' and artists' associations cannot put democracy into practice, then what governmental office or organization can do it for them? Our leaders should not resolve to act in the capacity of officials; instead they should resolve to act as well-meaning teachers and encouraging friends. The Party works through them to unify and show its concern for creative labor, academic research, and the living conditions of writers and artists. The Party works through our associations to convey its policy to authors and artists, at the same time allowing writers and artists to reflect their wishes and demands to the Party; these associations are not intended to suppress the initiative of artists and writers in the Party's name.

I call for unity built on the foundation of "letting a hundred flowers bloom, letting a hundred schools of thought contend." We must put a stop to attacks, retaliation, ostracism, and harsh treatment directed at those who hold dissenting opinions. There is absolutely no unity worthy of mention between a judge and the accused. Let us resolutely resist the sort of "unity" which in the past has been brought into being under the clubs of a certain few. They think that anyone who holds up his arms to shield his head is opposed to unity, while those who try to wrest the clubs from their hands are crazed advocates of insubordination and treason.

I call for minimal working conditions for artists and writers. Irrespective of which writers are labeled "eulogizers" or "back-stabbers," I would venture to say that some writers have committed "back-stabbing" in rooms furnished with red carpets. I have been to the homes of the most famous Chinese writers, but I have yet to see one that was carpeted. Many writers live in cramped quarters. Some writers who are renowned both here and abroad must consult with their wives and children every evening in order to reach a reasonable agreement on the use of their only table. This is the present status of men who for many years have been said to belong to the "mental aristocracy."

I call for concern over the nurturing of young writers. In recent years quite a few talented young writers have appeared, but there are no vehicles for the dissemination of most of their works, or they must resort to publication in mimeographed periodicals. Though certain problems still exist in their thought and writings, they have demonstrated their talent. They are seldom approached by people in literary circles, who find their thought "frightening." Their thought was not frightening from birth; rather, it is the product of a frightening era. I can predict that many excellent writers will appear among them, because most of them live at the grassroots level, have courage, and know how to think for themselves. We mustn't take them lightly; we should understand and guide them. Most young writers now active in the literary world are at least thirty-five years of age. For the sake of the future of Chinese literature, we must have an eye for what lies ahead! Whether we like it or not, the future belongs to the young. Do not block out the strengths and good points of our young writers and look only at their weaknesses. It is utterly mistaken to train young writers not to develop independent thinking and unique language. The more you loosen up control over this field, the sooner young writers will mature.

We are laborers. We serve the people through creative labor. I call for the protection, support, and encouragement of industrious laborers! I denounce the thieves and gangmasters of the literary world! I denounce slackness! I denounce those who concoct rumors! Last of all, I call for courageous action! Without courage there can be no breakthrough; without breakthrough there can be no literature!

Translated by Denis C. Mair
(Kaipi shehuizhuyi wenyi fanrong de xin shiqi)

7

OUR RESPONSIBILITY

Wang Meng

Ours was the first generation of youth in new China. Many of us joined in the people's revolutionary struggle at an early age. We strove to bring the light to those dark times so that the brilliance of the Party could be made even more brilliant. "The rising sun drives away the cold and the dark" was our favorite song lyric, for it echoed what was in our hearts.

For those of us who began to write at this time, literature and revolution seemed inseparable. Literature beckoned us to use truth, goodness, and beauty to resist all that was false, evil, and vulgar, and it led us onto the path of revolution. Revolution fired our youth, enriched and illuminated our lives, and inspired us to pick up the pen. We sang the praises of the red flag and the public squares, of the militia and the youth corps, and of the workers regulating the Huai River and the warriors constructing the Qinghai-Xizang Highway. Our admiration stretched all the way from the boats of the Southern Lakes to the lights of the Yan'an caves.

As we grew up, our observations and experiences became the natural basis of our sincere love for the Party, embracing both a youthful idealism and a number of impractical demands. When we saw the negative aspects of life, we passed on our immature observations and the fruits of our ponderings to the Party and the people. Just as the newborn calf does not fear the tiger, we too were naive, reckless, and, at times, ridiculous, but we were never disloyal, avaricious, fawning, or obsequious, nor were we forced to be on the defensive before the Party organization and leadership.

We were too young then, not yet rid of our childishness and lacking sufficient experience and preparation when asked to reflect reality and march off to the front lines of life. We deserved rebuke for failing to comprehend the power of the pen and for being unaware that, in order to speak the truth for the people, we had to pay a price and undergo all sorts of trials, requiring both an iron will and a crystal-clear character.

Over the past twenty years or more, we, the first generation of young writers in New China, have been extremely fortunate to experience the joy of "liberation" twice — once in 1949 and again during the past three years. How can we fail to be moved as we remember Comrades Mao Zedong, Zhou Enlai, and Zhu De? How can we fail to be moved as we give heartfelt thanks to Comrades Hua Guofeng, Ye Jianying, and Deng Xiaoping? Ours is a generation nurtured by the Party. The ultra-leftists did their utmost to destroy our flesh-and-blood relationship with the Party, branding us "anti-Party" and enemies of the Party, and driving us from the Party. But our intimate bond with the Party could not be severed! We belong to the Party! The Party's image will always brighten our lives! Even while we were suffering the most, our hearts were with the Party. On the first day that we were allowed to take up our pens again, our initial shouts of joy proclaimed our fervent love, trust, and loyalty to the Party, while we hated, cursed, and condemned the true enemies of the Party, the poisonous bacteria that tried to harm the Party. Were we to kneel before these enemies and poisonous bacteria and eulogize them? That is sheer lunacy! To praise such people would be a betrayal of the Party!

In recalling the past, we should not dwell on sentimentalism or personal resentments. We must regard the Party's setbacks as though they were our own. It is far more important to heal our motherland's wounds than to brood over our own personal scars. We can only hope that history will portray persons and events from the past as they truly were, that our experiences will be remembered and that the dues our fathers, brothers, and we ourselves paid for our current knowledge will not have been in vain. We have good reason to demand that the next generation of writers and readers and the Chinese masses meet with a better fate than ourselves. We need to firmly announce that we will not allow what happened to us to ever occur again.

"Solidarity can overcome calamity." The storms of the past twenty years have taught us quite a bit. Many of us have spent much of this time in the countryside, united in manual labor with poor and middle peasants and with ordinary laborers. We will now be tested under new conditions; we must stand with the people and act as their spokesmen.

The pressing needs of the people are to increase production, raise the standard of living, and realize the Four Modernizations, for our people are still very poor. At the same time, however, we need to raise our cultural level, enrich our literary and artistic lives, and overcome ignorance and backwardness step by step. The destruction caused by Lin Biao and the Gang of Four created a spiritual famine among the people; the most devastating and fearful effects were in the inability to nurture young talent. We now have a responsibility to produce more and better novels, poems, films, plays, music, and paintings.

Our people have come to not only dislike but despise excessive bureaucracy, the special privileges mentality, unjust practices, formulism, and empty words. It is our job to see life's contradictions for what they are. We must act as the people's spokesmen, expressing their anger and eliminating that which is incompatible with the nature of the Party, socialism, and the Four Modernizations.

The people need writers who will speak the truth, follow their bidding, and do right by them. The people also need writers and artists whose positive outlook and well-adjusted lives will help them enjoy that which is beautiful in life. What workers, peasants, and soldiers do not need is habitually simplistic "eulogizing." A steelworker drenched in sweat standing before a blast furnace doesn't need "eulogizing" as much as he does a cold drink. Under the pernicious influence and cruel oppression of the Gang of Four, "eulogizing" was no different from administering an anesthetic when what was needed was a call to arms and instruction on how to struggle on to victory. Since workers, peasants, and soldiers never became addicted to this incessant "eulogizing," it was only the ambitious opportunists of the Jiang Qing clique who couldn't survive without their daily fix of "eulogizing." Don't try to tell the workers, peasants, and soldiers that they need this kind of "eulogizing"!

Naturally, the people also have no need of excessive moaning and wailing, empty chatter, and meaningless gesticulating. As masters of life, Party affairs, and the nation, writers have a high level of responsibility to set things down as they see them, to use their works and words for the benefit of the people and for the good of peaceful unity and the Four Modernizations. The people are dauntless, composed, and patient. Writers need to bend a little, to join with the people in facing reality, and to join with the Party in facing difficulties, troubles, and problems. We must use our pens to assist in resolving these difficulties, troubles, and problems and not exacerbate them. We cannot afford to be dispassionate observers, but we must not be critical for the sake of criticism or go out of our way to be "stimulating." After ten calamitous and disruptive years, the pressing need of the people is for stability, unity, and rejuvenation. Our literature, together with art, needs to act as a bugle, a bayonet, and a hand grenade, as well as a microscope, a telescope, and an X-ray machine in order to link up with and enrich the people's hearts and spirits, like a mellow wine or fine tea. This great responsibility must not be taken lightly.

With this in mind, I hope that writers will reach out beyond their own literary circles and get to know workers, peasants, soldiers, clerks, teachers, prospectors, policemen, and others. We should also befriend leading cadres and those working at the grass-roots level in the trade unions, Youth League, and women's associations, as well as those involved in political and organizational work. We need to reduce the current gap in concepts and views between ideological workers and practical workers, and to increase our personal sense of realism and the realism in our works. Our pens will be employed to their maximum effectiveness when our works and voices are more accurate and more persuasive.

Our responsibility to the people and to the Party is the same — to write and speak the truth. Our literature is the literature of the Party and every one of our works and reputations reflects on the Party. Lies and deceptions serve only to destroy the reputation of the Party and of literature. They will be transparent no matter how well they are concealed under the flowery phrasings of "leftism." If we ignore or cover up the truth, we are cheating the people and the Party, which can only result in harm to the nation and to the people. Since the smashing of the Gang of Four, a large number of works have reflected life more truthfully, more extensively, and more incisively, helping to restore and further the Party's literary reputation. These initial signs of success should be treasured highly, and our renewal of literary activity must not be allowed to return down the dead-end of "leftism," where life is whitewashed and counterfeited.

We must now be bold in our pursuit of art, in creating and breaking through to novel ways. Every writer and every work is unique, so writers must strive to be creative; without creativity there can be no literature. We must be loyal to our own styles and souls, giving expression to our true thoughts and emotions. We must create bolder and freer artistic images, but should not allow these images to conflict with the accurate reflection of life. Literature is a spiritual activity that deals especially with people's inner worlds and spiritual lives. Without an active spiritual freedom, there can be no literature. Our writers must be sincere and bold, thoroughly using their creativity to cultivate artistic novelty; by promoting experimentation and praising that which breaks new ground, they will not be afraid of failure. We must oppose slavish imitation and the temptation to follow the crowd, and work toward eliminating the churning out of works that all appear to come out of a single model. We must guard against "playing it safe," literary opportunism, and the absurd reasoning that seeks "proper politics at the expense of strengthening one's art."

In order to realize the great responsibility the Party has handed us in this new historical era and to accomplish our historical mission, we need troops that are strong, vigorous, and capable of fighting the good fight on the literary front. Increasing literary productivity and replenishing it with new energy is of the utmost urgency. Following the smashing of the Gang of Four, a good number of notable writers have attracted attention. Compared to those of us who began writing in the fifties, these writers are, on the average, older and more mature intellectually and artistically. The ten years of the Cultural Revolution gave them time to think, explore, and prepare themselves; the fact that much of the superior writing of the past three years has come from their pens is no accident. Many amateur writers are now emerging or are about to emerge. We hope that the writers who comprise this new force will be encouraged and supported as they go on to brave new battles and earn their successes.

Of course, compared to members of the older generation, many of whom are here today, we are considered young. One cause for concern, however, is that our young and middle-aged writers are lacking in culture and knowledge compared to the elder generation. In order to implement the Four Modernizations and create an even higher level of socialist literature, we must try to catch up as quickly as possible.

Lu Xun and Guo Moruo have already left us. Lao She and Zhao Shuli have, unfortunately, also passed on. Following the calamity of the past ten years, we are lucky to still have the aged and esteemed Mao Dun, Ba Jin, Cao Yu, Yao Xueyin, and many other elder writers and artists. While we are delighted by this, their white hairs only serve to remind us of our own responsibilities.

The trials of the past ten years have shown that the people of China are a vigorous and tenacious people and that the Chinese Communist Party is a strong and indestructible Party. Our generation, educated by the Party and influenced by the spirit of the people, is also tenacious and indestructible. Having come through an arduous process, the majority of us, contrary to the calculations of foreign visitors, are not pessimistic, dejected, degenerate, or discouraged by any "lingering fears." We stand determined to work long and hard, to write more and better works, to scale the summits of literature and art, and, as new China's first generation of young writers, to contribute to the literary profession.

Translated by Stephen Horowitz
(Wenyibao, 1979, Nos. 11–12)

8

A FEW WORDS IN DEFENSE OF NEW POETRY AND THE LITERARY AND ART CONTINGENT

Ke Yan

After the fall of the Gang of Four I took part in a number of con-
ferences — science, finance and trade, education — so that I could
do features on some of the participants. When those outstanding
scientists, money managers, or educators rejoiced, shed tears, or
sobbed like children, I found myself doing the same. Every time
this happened I thought to myself: When will there be a conference
for writers and artists so that we, too, can rejoice over the destiny
of a new literature and art, over the destiny of our great motherland, and also cry to our hearts' content in each other's arms?

I don't know why, but after the fall of the Gang of Four I began to
cry easily. And it wasn't only I. It seemed that everybody else
was like this, especially some of the elders over sixty. It seemed
that those who were older, who were more tried and tested in the
Revolution, who never used to cry, now cried more easily. This,
I thought to myself, occurred because, during the rule of the Gang
of Four, anger and hatred had muffled our tears. During those
days we loved, hated, struggled, looked around with wide-open eyes,
and suppressed our tears, letting them flow only in our hearts.
Now that the Gang of Four has been ousted, and as we take a good
look at our dear motherland, as we share the people's every joy and
pain, we can let our tears flow freely, tears of the fighter, and the
child.

I was going to come to this meeting and have a good cry. I was
going to throw myself into the arms of the veteran writers and artists, and cry; to stroke the prematurely white hair of those of my
own generation, and cry; to hold the disabled limbs of my brothers
and sisters who were tortured and humiliated for following a non-
existent "black line in literature and art," and cry. Didn't the at-
tendees at last year's Expanded Session of the National Committee
of the Federation of Literary and Art Circles break into tears at

the sight of us and say, "Of all the meetings that have been held, yours is the saddest to the eye. You don't look like a combat battalion, but a hospital full of wounded...."

Yet, as we hold this conference today, I don't feel like crying any more. This conference was postponed so many times that all the other fields of work had moved forward with great strides and are already holding victory and award-giving meetings. We're so far behind that there's no time to give way to emotions. At this gathering of forces I hear not only the clarion call to march but the sound of running footsteps. What's more, so many of us are still alive! We are firmer, stronger, and more determined than ever to fight on. Yes, the Gang of Four was ruthless beyond words, but we are stronger than they. "The hair, unable to stand the test of time, has indeed turned white, but — the heart has not turned white, the blood has not turned white...." We've not only weathered the long, bloody night under the Gang of Four, but we still have the strength to go on singing at the top of our voices in this bright springtime!

How can we make our songs more forceful? As one still learning to write verse, I would like to make three points in connection with poetry.

1. A FEW WORDS IN DEFENSE OF NEW POETRY

In the last three years much progress has been made in all forms of literature and art. Stage plays, short stories, reportages, and cartoons have consistently led the way. In comparison poetry does not seem to have made very significant progress. Still I don't agree with those who say that poetry has nothing to show at all. Especially new poetry. The very mention of it draws snorts of contempt and such comments as, "New poetry? I wouldn't read it if you gave me a hundred dollars!" There's the story of the bookstore salesclerk who didn't want to get a book of poems down from the shelf for his customer.

"That's poetry," he was quoted as saying.

"Let me have a look," the customer said.

"That's poetry!" the clerk raised his voice, meaning that the person wouldn't buy it even if he looked at it.

But the customer happened to be a poet. "That's just what I want."

The irritated salesclerk pulled a volume from the shelf and slapped it down on the counter in front of the customer....

Is this a true story? Yes. But this is only one side of the issue, and the Gang of Four is mainly responsible for it. For ten years the Gang used poetry as a weapon for seizing Party power. They had people compile such volumes as Nursery Rhymes from a Xisi Primary School and Selected Poems from Xiaojinzhuang, and organized "poetry competitions" in every conceivable place. People were made to recite poems they never wrote, and a lot of the poems were trash. There was even a compilation called One Hundred Most Commonly Used Verses. A sample verse reads:

"X X X, a big rotten egg, we won't rest until we strike him down, then trample him underfoot so he can never rise again."

X X X could be changed at will. It could be a proper name, or a common term like "democratic personage" or "landlords' restitution corps" or whatever. It could be an ancient or contemporary person, a Party or non-Party member, a military or nonmilitary person, an enlisted man or a marshal — whomever they wanted struck down at the time.

Artistically they were terrible lines too. "The great road is endless/ The pines are evergreen" or "The east wind blows ten thousand li/ Sea waves rise to the sky" or "Sea waves rise/ Red flags unfurl/ The Standard-Bearer* does this and that/ Loud singing soars to the clouds." Lines like these filled the book market so that a lot of young people thought poetry writing was the easiest thing in the world. They just picked up a pen and came up with hundreds or thousands of lines like "Oh how arduous and how glorious/ We are criticizing Lin Biao and Confucius/ We will occupy the field of history/ A thousand years of history is for us to evaluate," or "We vie to take the front line in criticizing Lin Biao and Confucius/ We're here to comment on the Legalists and criticize the Confucians/ We follow the Standard-Bearer and go into battle/ And fight for bright red happiness." Gibberish and wrongly written words filled the pages. As long as a poem praised the "Standard-Bearer" and condemned the "capitalist roaders" it was considered

---

*Standard-Bearer here refers to Jiang Qing, leader of the Gang of Four — Tr.

revolutionary and would get printed, and its writer would be on his way up the ladder. The whole thing was bad for the education of the young and killed the reader's appetite for poetry. The name of poetry became mud. Indeed, comrades in the poetry circles have a tremendous amount of work to do to set things right. This, I must still say, is only one side of the issue.

The other side is that a great many poems have reached deep into people's hearts. These poems are being read widely and have moved the people as never before. Ours has always been a nation of poetry. Since ancient times poets have written poems to which friends replied, using the same rhyme sequence. We all know the ancient story of Zuo Si, whose poetry was copied so widely that the price of paper in Luoyang soared. Then times changed. This tradition seemed to have been kept only among the literary people, the intellectuals. In recent years, however, the tradition has been revived and on a much wider scope than before. The revival shows the enormous power of poetry, particularly new poetry. I will give two examples.

One is about the poems from Tian An Men Square. I needn't go into this in detail, as we all lived through that event. As soon as the poems appeared in the Square, people hurried to tell one another about them, copy them, pass them around. They wept at hearing the poems recited and shouted their praises. Though threatened by beatings and jail, pressured by investigations and arrests, they did not knuckle under or destroy their collections of the poems, but went right on passing them around and memorizing them. All kinds of methods were used to preserve the poems — hiding the copies in walls, winding them in balls of yarn, burying them underground, committing them to memory. Many families stayed awake nights, grandpas waking grandsons, parents waking children, to say, "Child, you have a good memory; memorize these." As each line was recited and listened to closely, tears flowed. By word of mouth the poems spread, widely, in a manner unprecedented in Chinese history. Why? Because these poems expressed the people's pent-up wrath at the Gang of Four and their deep love for Premier Zhou.

"The long wide avenue is hushed as still water/ One million people stand without uttering a word/ Silently, wordlessly, they all lower their proud heads/ There can be heard only the north wind whistling and people sobbing/ Even as tears stream down cold cheeks...."

"Please, oh please accept this plain white flower of ours/ It may be crude/ But it is made with true hearts and pure hands/ And it is dedicated to you!"

These simple lines, filled with the tears of millions, moved the hearts of millions.

> China is no longer the China of the past,
> The people are not to be made fools of.
>
> ....
>
> What we want is true Marxism-Leninism.
> If we do not explode from silence,
> We will perish in silence!
>
>   * * *
>
> In our grief we hear the demons shriek,
> While we weep the wolves and jackals laugh.
> Tears streaming, we come to mourn the great man,
> Heads raised, we unsheath our swords.

People lit up with joy on reading these poems, recited them in loud voices, ran to spread them, for in them they saw the awakening of the younger generation, the awakening of the people; in them they saw hope for China. Is there anyone sitting here today who was not swept into that torrent of poems, who did not write or copy some, or memorize some, or send some as gifts to relatives and friends or even to strangers?

Another example is the titled poetry recitals we held, recitals entitled "The Struggle for Truth," and "Learn from Martyr Zhang Zhixin," and others. We asked both veteran and young poets to write about the heroes of the Tian An Men Incident and the Nanking Incident. There are Ai Qing's "On the Crest of the Waves," Zhang Zhimin's "Following the People's Mandate," Bai Hua's "Sunlight — No One Must Monopolize It," Shao Yanxiang's "To Comrade Dou Shoufang," Han Han's "Struggle for Truth," and many others. These political lyric poems run to at least three or four hundred lines and would take twenty or thirty minutes to recite. At first some of us were afraid that audiences might not have the patience to sit through the long recitations. What actually happened was that the audience listened attentively, almost with bated breath, often interrupting the recitation with applause after two or three lines. Some seemingly simple lines were greeted with thunderous applause. About the hero in the poem "On the Crest of the Waves" the poet wrote: "His poem was pasted on the east face of the Monument.... This young worker

was arrested/ The place, beneath Lenin's portrait/ The time, two
days before Qing Ming 1976, at twelve midnight...." Plain lines,
but greeted with roars from the audience. Then: "All policies
must be translated into facts/ All wrongs must be righted/ Even
those long turned to dust must be rehabilitated...." The applause
was deafening! The entire indoor stadium shook. Why? Because
these lines depict a familiar scene typified by the poet: A young
worker, out to defend the name of Premier Zhou and worried over
the fate of his country, wrote a poem full of love for his country
and pasted it on the east face of the Monument to the People's
Heroes, in the most sacred of places in China, Tian An Men Square.
For this he was arrested and the place of arrest was beneath the
portrait of Lenin! What more is needed to pinpoint the issue! Then
poet Ai Qing shouted what was in the hearts of millions. His poem
was written with his own blood and tears and the people's blood and
tears. Therefore his shouts were the shouts of the people.

Or take "Sunlight — No One Must Monopolize It." When the reciter went from

"One word lays bare the truth"

to

"Some people consider themselves owners of truth/ How can
truth be any one person's private property!/ In vain they try to
rake in high interests through extortion/ Like misers practicing
usury/ No!/ Truth is wealth belonging to all the people/ Truth,
like sunlight, cannot be monopolized by anyone!" The audience
laughed, roared approval, then broke into stormy applause.

The reciter went on:

"The true defenders of the standard are the people/ To defend the
standard, the people let their bleached bones pile high as the mountain/
To defend the standard, the people let their hot blood flow like the river/
No one has the right to appoint himself the standard-bearer."

Prolonged applause. Why? Because the poet not only uses artistic, poetic, and forceful language to help his audience deepen their
understanding that practice is the sole criterion for determining
truth, but he expresses what was in people's hearts so incisively
that the words struck a responsive chord and stimulated the reasoning mind, calling on the listeners to rise and join the fight. I
don't know how to describe the feverish scene. I only know I was
deeply moved. It was a profound education.

It was the same with the recital, "Learn from Martyr Zhang
Zhixin." Presenting Lei Shuyan's "A Tiny Blade of Grass Is

Singing," the reciter related, "The wind says/ Forget her/ I have
buried the crime with dust!/ The rain says/ Forget her/ I have
cleansed the humiliation with tears!/... Only a tiny blade of grass
is still singing/ So mournfully on starless nights/ So stirringly at
scorching high noons.... She/ Was shot to death/ Fell to the
ground, right beside her mother/ Who gave her life and brought
her up...." Waves of sobbing in the audience. "I am ashamed
that I/ A Communist Party member/ Am no better than a tiny blade
of grass/ Who lets her blood flow into its arteries/ Night and day/
Singing unceasingly... Let me keep awake!/ Let me keep awake!/
Living in the doldrums/ Is more lamentable than death/ Living in
ignorance/ Is worse than a pig's life!" As if whipped across the
heart, the audience shuddered, then broke into a hurricane of applause that went on and on.

There were many other poetry recitals. Most of the presentations
were of new poetry. As soon as a recital announcement appeared
in the newspapers, people started lining up at midnight to buy tickets. The police had to be called in to maintain order. Nobody paid
these people a hundred dollars to come to the recitals. In fact,
many young people saved their breakfast money or bus fare to buy
the tickets. When a recital was over, they did not leave, but crowded
the back doors of the theater or stadium asking if they could copy
the poems. Some went home and mailed us money, asking us to
print copies to send to them.

Here I've only talked about poems presented at recitals. The
fact is, fine poems by both veteran and young poets published in
newspapers and magazines in the past three years are too numerous to name. I am only trying to show that poetry, new
poetry, can be appreciated by readers and listeners. As long as
the poet thinks as the people do, feels as the people do, speaks for
the people, makes his poems the voice of the times, then his poetry
is dynamic and the poet becomes the poeple's own kith and kin.

We will try hard to be poets like that. We hope that comrades in
the fields that are way ahead of us will help and criticize us, not
condemn or sneer at us. Don't dwell on stories like "That's poetry"
but join us in clearing away the baleful influence of the Gang of
Four. I hope that comrades who are critics will study the problem
of poetry writing, make an effort to get acquainted with writers of
new poetry, publish commentaries to guide poetry writing, and in
this way contribute to the flourishing of poetry. This is the first
point I want to make.

2. OUR CONTINGENT

In our contingent there are elders who began warring against imperialism and feudalism as early as the May Fourth New Culture Movement; veteran soldiers who had followed the Communist Party through hails of gunfire during the various revolutionary periods; middle-aged writers who grew up with the new China; and young people who came to the fore after the fall of the Gang of Four. We're a mighty contingent, no less than a million in all.

How should we evaluate this million-strong contingent? There had been an evaluation before the founding of the People's Republic. Chairman Mao stated clearly in his 1942 "Talks at the Yan'an Forum on Literature and Art" that this was a cultural contingent of the Communist Party. At the First Congress of Writers and Artists we were called "People's Artists." Yet somehow or other, as time went by, as criticism, repudiation, and struggles went on year after year, things changed, and finally we all became "bourgeois intellectuals." We were turned over to the bourgeoisie — lock, stock, and barrel. By the time of the Cultural Revolution we had sunk even lower. We were "reactionaries in the arts and letters," "monsters and demons" [class enemies of all descriptions — Tr.], "traitors and special agents," "stinking old ninths [stinking intellectuals — Tr.]," and "disciples and followers of the black line in literature and art." We were expelled from the ranks of the people and condemned to "the other register" [listing disreputable people — Tr.] so that Jiang Qing and company could "reorganize the ranks."

But the people thought differently. When some of those in this contingent were sent into exile, one after another, the people took them in, one by one, silently protecting and taking care of them. When the entire contingent was purged (with the exception of a very few), the people took them all into their vast embraces, sharing their anger and their agony, an emotional experience that helped the people see Jiang Qing and company for what they really were.

The veteran proletarian revolutionaries thought differently too. Eighteen years ago I had the good fortune to attend the Guangzhou Meeting. In a talk at this meeting our respected and beloved Premier Zhou said: "This contingent of intellectuals is the people's own contingent, a contingent of intellectuals belonging to the proletariat and nurtured by the Party." Answering the accusation of some extreme leftists, Marshal Chen [Yi] said, taking off his cap, "I now remove the label of 'bourgeoisie' from your heads. I take off my cap in salutation to you. From now on, if anybody should dare say that you are a part of the bourgeoisie and try to attack you, denounce you, or put labels on you, you come to me...." My comrades and I cheered and jumped with joy, announcing confidently wherever we went: "We're not outsiders. We're the Party's own children."

But I was too young then to understand the weight of these words. And of course I never dreamed that the day would come when we could never again rouse Premier Zhou and Marshal Chen, even though we cried until we were hoarse. I never dreamed that even they would be branded as "bourgeoisie," as "the biggest capitalist roaders in the Party," and would die from persecution, from frustration and anger.

But history, ever merciless, sooner or later shows things as they really are. After the fall of the Gang of Four, at the Conference of Scientists, the Party declared that intellectuals were mental laborers who were a part of the working class. We were returned to the ranks of the people. At this meeting Comrade Deng Xiaoping, on behalf of the Party Central Committee, reiterated that ours was a fine contingent. "The literary and art circles," he said, "have made significant achievements. Writers and artists should be trusted, loved, and respected by the Party and the people." Only this time I did not cheer or jump up and down. I listened with meditative tears in my eyes, because I was no longer young. After more than twenty years of stress and strain and ten years of holocaust, drenched in blood and tears, I now understood the weight of these words. More than that, I was forced to ponder: Why did it take the Party and the people such a long time and so much bloodshed to reach this simple truth, this undisputed fact?

It is as simple as one plus one equals two. This contingent may have shortcomings, may have made mistakes, but it is a loyal and energetic contingent, working with one heart and mind. It should never have needed to be proven.

I'd heard the story of the artist, living in a hole of a room in winter, who painted a window filled with lovely spring flowers. I'd heard stories of film and stage artists persisting in practicing their skills every day, even though the beatings they received had damaged their voices or broken their backs or legs. I'd heard the story of the novelist who, returning from "struggle meetings," washed the dirt off his face but, not stopping to wipe the spittle from his clothes, continued to meditate on his novel. Now allow me to tell you stories about some poets.

During the days when some people were duped into taking the law into their own hands, one of our comrades received a brutal beating at the hands of some of these people. When he was brought back to the "bull pen" [a temporary place of detention for all those subjected to investigation — Tr.], the poet Guo Xiaochuan was lying in bed sick. Tears welled up in Guo's eyes when he saw the blood on his comrade's face. How he longed to rush up and hold the wounded comrade in his arms, as he had done so many times in the years of war, to wash the wounds and say a few comforting words! But, as we all know, that was prohibited. They were all being watched closely. Defying the rules would only bring more trouble and more beatings. Without changing his position, Xiaochuan began tracing words on his own chest with his finger.... He kept doing it until he caught the other comrade's attention. The comrade, also without moving his body, followed the tracing with his eyes. He soon realized that Xiaochuan was saying to him, "Go on living! Go — on — living!" That comrade lived, but Xiaochuan has left us, much too soon. Yet Xiaochuan is not dead. His poems live on among us. Here's one:

> The fighter can cease singing for a while,
> But his voice will never become hoarse.
> The fighter can close his eyes for a while,
> But he will never go blind.
> The fighter has a fighter's love: undyingly loyal,
>   beautiful as a painting...
> It cannot be expressed with voices, only voices
>   without "voices"...

Every time I hear these lines I cannot hold back my grief, because I understand their meaning fully. I felt that the young comrade reciting them also understood their meaning fully.

> I know that there'll be a day when I will turn into smoke,
>   smoke that rises into the sky;
> Let it be like gunsmoke, heavy, very heavy with
>   the smell of gunpowder....

Remember, Xiaochuan wrote this poem when he was being closely watched and had absolutely no freedom. How precious is the loyalty of a fighter who, even when deprived of freedom, still longs to go amid gunsmoke and gunfire, to lay down his life in combat. Songs like this have been sung not only by Xiaochuan, such loyalty as expressed in his poem is possessed not by him alone. Xiaochuan is only one representative of our contingent. Let me recite another poem for you. It is called "The Tree at the Edge of the Cliff."

> We do not know what strange wind it was
> That blew that tree to the edge of the great prairie,
> Right to the cliff overhanging the deep ravine.
>
> The tree listens to the merriment in the faraway forests
> And the singing of running brooks down in the ravine.
> It stands there by itself,
> Lonely yet stubborn.
>
> The bent body of the tree
> Has the very shape of the wind.
> It seems about to fall into the ravine,
> Yet seems also ready to take wing and soar...

This poem is by Comrade Zeng Zhuo, who was detained for his implication in an "antirevolutionary" case and later sent to work on a farm for a dozen or more years. I've never met Comrade Zeng Zhuo and don't know much about his experience, but this little poem of his moves me deeply. Reading it, I not only hear the "wind" again but see the shapes the "wind" has left on the bodies of millions. Yet the hues of the tree are neither dim nor dark. Even as it is about to fall into the ravine it listens intently to the merriment in the forests, lifts its eyes to the blue sky and the sunlight, full of hope, ready to take wing and soar...

It is an image of agony, also an image of joy. This tree is in agony because it does not know why it has been blown to the edge of the cliff by this unknown, strange wind. It is joyous because even as it is about to perish it sends forth light in the darkness, sings amid pain, soars amid flames — no iron chains can lock up the wings or its heart and soul.

This is the image of not just one life, but countless lives. There are so many, many images like this in our contingent, strong and crystal clear, with deep thoughts embodied in agony!

There is the comrade who was sent to work in a factory as a form of punishment. He worked piously for many, many years and was actually named a ninth-grade worker by his worker-colleagues. (Eighth is the highest grade for industrial workers. Being called

ninth is a special commendation.) There are those comrades who
were sent to work on the farm as "criminals" but while there were
regarded as kith and kin by the peasants. There are those comrades in the theater who were made to move props around the stage
and were shifted from one "labor gang" to another for a whole decade, but who kept up their extensive reading night after night,
amassing strength for tomorrow. There are those comrades who
were made to labor under surveillance year after year, their families broken up in the meantime, but who kept on hammering out
verses even as they forged iron on the anvil. I want also to tell you
about one comrade who was branded a "rightist," purged from the
army, sent to the primeval forests in the Northeast to keep company with wild beasts. But for two decades he consistently behaved
in the tradition he was taught in the army. He never once informed
on anybody to his superiors, never wrote one sentence framing
others in the copious materials he was made to write, never said
one word to hurt the Party, never did anything harmful to the people. . . .

Can you call people like these bourgeois? Are there bourgeoisie
like these in the world?

After the fall of the Gang of Four, these falsely charged "rightists," "monsters and demons," "capitalist roaders," and "reactionary authorities" were rehabilitated. Most of them plunged right
back into work without a word of complaint. In the past three years
they've written a great many moving poems. They have shown
themselves to possess such talent, such intelligence, and such deep
feelings for the Party and the people that one young man, who in the
days of the Gang of Four had written poems denouncing "capitalist
roaders" and repudiating Deng Xiaoping, exclaimed in alarm: "Now
that these people are back, what's going to happen to us? . . . With
all the rightists acting like leftists, what will people think of us
leftists?"

What will people think? The mind of the people is a steelyard.
Rightists, leftists, ultra-leftists — history will accord each person
a proper place befitting his footprints. History is always fair and
just. The ten years of experience is a profound lesson. Those who
climbed onto the "leftist throne" by attacking and vilifying others
are only symbols of shame in the eyes of the people. Let us all
work honestly and try not to go against historical currents. Allow
me to recite a poem by the poet Wang Liaosheng. It describes our
entire contingent. It is titled "In Quest" and was published

by the magazine <u>Rain Threads</u>.

> Millions of searchers are constantly in quest,
> Blazing trails amid thistle and thorns;
> They wield broadswords and sabers
> Only because the ground underfoot is rough.

> . . . .

> Oh, searchers of twenty-two years ago,
> Are you still walking the earth or have you gone to rest?
> As long as the ship's hull is made of steel,
> It will not rot, nor will it stall midway.

> If no one is in search of anything,
> Then when will Truth ever be found?
> Let's just hope that those who suffer anguish for their quest,
> Will find comfort in finishing their performance of the last act.

> So many brilliant people had their burning flames extinguished,
> So many stars no longer shine as they did before;
> We're afraid to look back at history,
> Just one look will shock the mind and overwhelm the soul!

> But believe me, please believe me,
> As long as there is love there will be no debasement,
> Living, we'll search for the road to renascence for our motherland,
> Dead, our bodies will fill up the gullies and hollows of our motherland.

> Once sunlight floods the earth again,
> All who should come alive will come alive again;
> Oh stubborn, tenacious searchers,
> Living or dead, they cling to the pulse of love.

> The hair, unable to stand the test of time,
> Has indeed turned white, but —
> The heart has not turned white, the blood has not turned white,
> These we dedicate to the torrents of modernization!

> . . . .

> Even as the rolling waves are irresistible,
> The right to quest is inalienable;
> Let us hold high the searchers' sword
> And make the whole world look at China with new eyes!

This is a true description of our contingent — a contingent that is loyal, forward looking, invincible, above personal honor and humiliation, filled with a love for our country, and ready for combat at a moment's notice. This is a contingent nurtured by the Party and the people, a contingent of the proletariat's own writers and artists. Don't ever again brand us as "monsters" or "stinking old ninths" and don't ever again try to push us over to the side of the bourgeoisie. Whoever tries to do so is committing a crime against history. Besides, no one could succeed even if he tried!

3. A WORD TO THE LEADERS IN THE
LITERARY AND ART CIRCLES

When I say "a word" I mean "two points."

The first point: I hope that the leaders will lead in a positive way, not take a passive preventive attitude.

We are a socialist country. We should have as many writers and artists as there are stars on a clear summer night. There were times in our history when talented people came to the fore in huge numbers — in the twenties, the thirties, and the forties. At the First Young Writers Conference, held in the early days of the People's Republic, there were at least several hundred up-and-coming and very promising writers. But as time passed not many remained as writers, and we all know why. Nevertheless I suggest that the leaders review this situation from a theoretical point of view and determine the reasons for it. Certainly it is not going to be easy, and not every leader will be able to do it. But it should and must be done. Whoever is able to do it will not repeat past mistakes and will win the people's trust.

Our Writers Association does not support professional writers. It is said that when there are writers, they become targets of attack and could be sent to labor camps on the slightest excuse. Think about it, comrade leaders. How many of the writers sent to labor camps were really enemies? How many should have been sent down as criminals? We know that some organizations followed a given percentage when branding rightists. If those organizations did not have these professional writers, then the one, two, or three percent [of rightists] would most probably have included certain leaders. Wasn't it also true that some leaders were against branding so many people as "antirevolutionaries" and "rightists" and so were themselves branded as "middle-rightists" and transferred to other positions, or were themselves branded as rightists?

The modern theater has been in the forefront ever since the removal of the Gang of Four. Aside from the efforts of comrades in the theater, the achievements are inseparable from the fact that the theatrical groups have for decades maintained a professional contingent.

Of course, when there is a contingent, there must be leadership. It is the job of leaders to study the problem of writers trying to gain experience in the thick of life, the problem of writers re-molding their world outlook, the problem of helping writers improve their professional skills and seeing that they have the conditions to produce good works ... and a string of other problems. But isn't this what leading comrades are supposed to do? What else should they do? Attack others? Determine what can and cannot be writ-ten? Give stupid instructions on things they know little about? Lord it over others in their capacity as high officials? I don't know about other things but I do know that, since the founding of the Peo-ple's Republic, the greatest concentrations of literary talent were found in the following places: the Literary Institute run by Ding Ling, Gong Mu, and others; the Kunming Military Area; and the Nanking Military Area. This is not to say that other places did not produce good writers, but these three places have produced the greatest numbers. People have come to the fore or disappeared from the scene in the last thirty years, but many of the most active comrades in the literary circles today were trained at these places years ago. I suggest that the leaders study the experience of these places and, of course, draw whatever lessons can be learned from them.

We have started a new Long March, the march to modernize our country. Professional people in every field are being tested to as-sess their capabilities. As professionals we hope that the leaders in our field will strengthen leadership over us and continue to test us and assess our work — our depth of feeling for the people, how well we have remolded our world outlook, the level of our political and ideological understanding, the quality of our products, how well we have done in preserving unity ... these and many other things. We, on our part, as we exercise our democratic rights, will also examine and assess the work of the leaders, to see if they are carrying out the correct line, how they're doing in understanding and implementing policies, to see whether their leadership is in keeping with the laws of the arts, how they're implementing the "Double Hundred" policy ... We hope that in future summing-up and evaluation meetings we will hear the leaders speak about how they have expanded the ranks of writers and artists, what they have

done toward promoting literature and art, which association or
which leaders have helped in the production of good works and the
training of fine new talents, and how many. We will not want to hear
how many imaginary enemies and "white and professional" examples
[those who are professionally outstanding but politically unreliable
— Tr.] they have uncovered, or the percentage of people they have
sent to "reform through labor"...

The second point: I hope that the leaders will treasure their
rank-and-file soldiers. I have said that ours is a fine contingent,
but that is not to say that there are no extreme individualists among
us, people whose minds have been deeply poisoned by the Gang of
Four and people of flimsy moral fiber. I therefore propose that the
leaders go among the masses to find out at first hand what's going
on at the grass roots. Don't listen to one side only; don't act on
assumptions. Treasure in particular those who really work at their
professions, not the flatterers, informers, and slanderers. When
you receive a report with such information as "my name is X X X,
age X X, family origin X X, political status X X; I have discovered
that a certain publication is a 'black flag' publication, an antirevolutionary publication, that X X's writing is a vicious attack...," be on
your guard, look into it carefully, handle it with caution, and find
out if the information is true. When the Gang of Four was in power,
it bought slanderers and informers with high prices so that it became common practice to send in "private reports" on others in
return for self-promotion. The Gang of Four has been ousted but
this deplorable practice they started has yet to be rooted out.
Therefore, respected comrade leaders, beware of people with a
price. Of course we will continue to unite with these people, but
uniting with them is not the same as buying them over with high
prices. Only when you cease buying people with high prices will
there be fewer such people. Historical experience merits our attention. A person who spent twenty years writing a book has been
known to be totally discredited by someone who spent two hours
writing a report with false charges. We will not allow this kind of
history to be repeated. The people will not permit it!

Historical experience also tells us that a hundred flowers will not
bloom under clubs and whips. Literature and art will thrive only under
correct leadership from the Party, with the practice of democracy in
the arts, with the implementation of the "Double Hundred" policy, and
with writers and artists working with a high sense of responsibility toward the people and the Party. Leadership is the key to all this.

If the leaders in the literary and art circles can truly be like the Party Central Committee and truly recognize the fact that ours is a fine contingent, tried and tested, worthy of the trust, love, and respect of the Party and the people; if the leaders can truly respect the laws of the arts, practice democracy in the arts, and correctly implement the Party's principles and policies; and if every one of us professional people can make stringent demands on ourselves, continue to establish closer ties with the masses of the people, work hard in the study of Marxism-Leninism–Mao Zedong Thought, serve the people diligently, and dare to scale the peaks of the arts, then before long China will see a renaissance of its new literature and art. This contingent of writers and artists will live up to the expectations of our time and find its rightful place in history.

Let us unite and work with one heart and mind and give our all to promoting the flowering of a new literature and art, to the vigorous growth of our contingent of writers and artists.

Translated by Betty Ting
(Zhongguo wenxue yishu
gongzuozhe disici daibiao
dahui wenji)

9

SOME SUGGESTIONS CONCERNING LITERARY WORK

Chen Dengke

I

Originally I did not wish to say anything at the general meeting. To be candid, having pursued a literary career for thirty years, I have acquired some worldly wisdom, particularly after the tribulations of the Cultural Revolution. But after having listened to the reports by Comrades Deng Xiaoping, Hu Yaobang, and Zhou Yang, I find my mind churning once again; with this warm feeling in my heart, I cannot refrain from saying something. The words spoken by other comrades during the past two days have given me courage, and it is the valiant spirit of these comrades that has motivated me to mount this platform....

During the past three decades, Chinese literature has gone down a winding road; so have our writers. As far as I am concerned, during the 1940s, as I began to learn how to write under the guidance of seniors, I felt that I was very close to the people. Having been nurtured by the people, I wanted to pick up my pen and say what was in the people's hearts. I was in such a frame of mind when I wrote the novel Living Hell. I think all of us share the experience that, when one's work conveys the people's aspirations, one feels so much at ease. But as time went on, things began to change and a multitude of criticism campaigns imposed countless restrictions on writers. Whoever violated these restrictions was subjected to criticism and attack or deprived of his writing instruments or even his right of existence. Consequently, the writers dared not look at life squarely or reflect life truthfully.

In 1958, as the "boastful trend," the "communistic trend," and the anti-rightist campaign, which confounded right and wrong, were spreading throughout the nation, I wrote not to defend the people's interests but to follow others in distorting life, falsifying life, and deceiving the people. I even went so far as to attack those comrades who dared to reflect the people's sufferings. In the early 1960s, as the head of a work team, I went to the villages north of the Huai River and witnessed the disasters brought about by the "muddle-headed" policies in effect. People were suffering from hunger, dropsy, and death. I personally handled "special cases" one after the other. How could I not ponder over this? In the past, we fought and wrote for the liberation of the people. Now the people were suffering again, so shouldn't we have taken up our pens to cry out for them? Yet, what I could write were "The situation has greatly improved" and "The prospects are bright." How painful that was! I felt that I was betraying my conscience and the people.

In 1962, I revised Wind and Thunder out of a minimum sense of responsibility and to some degree reflected some of the people's suffering in the work. Because of this, the cap of "special agent" was personally bestowed upon me by Jiang Qing, and a prison term of more than five years was given to me. As a member of the Communist Party and a writer who was nursed to maturity by the Party and the people, I felt nothing fearful about being in prison. What was fearful was the fact that a communist writer, being imprisoned by the Communist Party, shackled and handcuffed, was required to wish Lin Biao eternal health as though it were a sutra-recitation and prayerlike ritual. If he had enjoyed eternal health, our nation would have perished. But, at the time, from one end of the country to the other, wasn't there a chorus of prayers? What a ridiculous tragedy it has been for our Party and for our people!...

II

I am of the opinion that today a new literary revolutionary movement is in the making. This new literary revolutionary movement began with the great revolutionary mass movement at Tian An Men Square on the Qingming Festival Day in 1976. Like the May Fourth Movement of 1919, which set in motion the New Culture Movement, it is another Chinese Renaissance.

The revolutionary mass movement on the Qingming Festival Day of 1976, in political terms, launched a fierce attack upon the feudalistic—fascist rule represented by the Gang of Four and, in organizational terms, firmly upheld the leadership of the Party and the true democratic movement of the socialist revolution; the weapons it used were wreaths, poems, recitations, and paintings — literature and the arts were given full play of their functions in combat. Poems from Tian An Men ought to be engraved in gold in our literary history. An outstanding characteristic of this literary revolutionary movement is that it has restored the realistic tradition. It is precisely because I have gone down a winding road in my creative life and precisely because I have undergone numerous painful experiences and lessons that I have become increasingly convinced that our literary work of today requires that we all promote realism. Since I am not a literary theoretician, I cannot offer any profound theories. But there has been a lingering doubt in my mind; that is to say, I have a problem, thus far unresolved, which I would like to present to you at this meeting to seek your advice.

During the three decades since the founding of our nation, there have been numerous major criticism campaigns in the field of literature and the arts, all of which were, of course, mounted against rightists. Since you are more familiar with these than I, I shall not dwell upon them here. What puzzles me is the fact that the themes of several criticism campaigns were aimed at arguments for and advocates of realism, as though realism and realistic depiction were representative of the rightist viewpoint. In the Summary [of the Forum on Literary and Art Works in the Armed Forces], concocted by Lin Biao and Jiang Qing, they regarded "realism — a broad avenue," "realistic depiction," and "intensification of realism," terms that represented purely academic arguments, as unpardonable major crimes to be arbitrarily hung around writers' necks. Even up to now, there has not been any authoritative article refuting this line justly and forcefully; it is as though the mere mention of realism meant exposure of the dark side of life or wreaking havoc by the rightists. This I do not understand. Does it mean that realism is our sworn "enemy"?

I am happy to see that, in spite of the fact that a number of topsy-turvy theoretical issues have not yet been given due clarification, in the area of creative works a number of novellas and short stories, movie scripts, and plays written in the realistic vein have emerged. The characteristics of these works are that they boldly expose the darkness of the rule of Lin Biao and the Gang of Four; boldly lift the covers off the bloody wounds of the people and society resulting from the catastrophe; and figuratively narrate a period of complex history under feudalistic—fascist rule during a socialist period, thus providing us with food for thought. Because such a group of works is leading the charge against the enemy lines, the great banner of realism has again been raised in the camp of revolutionary literature, and the styles of these writers are advancing toward all sorts of strictly forbidden areas. No longer are they mere mouthpieces for eulogizing someone's merits and virtues; no longer will they portray men as gods; no longer will they forcibly burden reality with mirages.

In the past, the field of literature and the arts was repeatedly opposed to formulism and jargonism, but whenever someone really explored the situation or tried to experiment with some creative work, he was immediately criticized and punished. I myself had just such a painful lesson. Were the works in Fresh Flowers Abloom Again not all regarded as poisonous weeds? Is this not the best proof? The Gang of Four epitomized formulism and jargonism and rather uniquely brought forth what is known as "models," advancing jargonism and formulism to their limits. Now and only now can we discard formulism and jargonism and truly restore the tradition of realism. The excellent works that have emerged in recent years have swept away the air of the Gang of Four and swept away formulism and jargonism. All this must be credited to the great strength of the literary tradition of realism.

Lin Biao and the Gang of Four ruled the nation for a decade. Is there anyone who can say that it was a bright period, as long as he did not shut his eyes and tell lies or if he was not one of their favorites, "kept men," or special emissaries, and who cared to look reality in the face? Then, why couldn't this be reflected in literature? To expose darkness or to sing the praises of brightness have never been absolutes. It is precisely because the writers are in pursuit of brightness that they ruthlessly expose darkness. It is precisely because they voice the inner thoughts of the people and reflect the livelihood of the people that these works have a certain degree of depth and are acceptable to the people. As I see it, they are realistic. Socialism absolutely does not permit the existence of fascism. Our Party has the boldness of vision to look reality in the face, to smash the Gang of Four, and to restore the democratic system socialism requires. Our veteran general, Comrade Ye Jianying, on behalf of the Party and the people, made a report on the thirtieth anniversary of the nation in which he pointed out with unreserved candor that the reign of Lin Biao and the Gang of Four was an "unprecedented catastrophe." This alone reflects the superiority and boldness of vision of socialism, the daring to expose our own contradictions, and the daring to rewrite history that has been distorted. Are not the characters and images penned by our writers the very details of history?

To be sure, I do not believe that realism is the be-all and end-all of this literary movement, but undoubtedly it is the mainstream.

In the spring of this year, a cold wind again blew from the "Left." Some comrades who were responsible for leading the work in literature and the arts did not wholeheartedly lend their support and guidance, but merely made idle gestures and even showed dislike for works that exposed the crimes of the Gang of Four, a fact that can only astound us. I am a relatively ignorant and uninformed person, but I have had an earful of their pronouncements. They were saying things like "the field of literature is still right-leaning," "the situation of 1956 has reappeared," "we have deviated from Chairman Mao's direction of literature and the arts," and "the nature of these works is to seize power." They also accused certain works of being "literature of the wounded," "exposé literature," "worse than counterrevolutionary tracts," etc. Even though most of these accusations were not published but were distributed as internal directives and documents, they spread like wildfire, for there was a group of people who drew their meal tickets from "campaigns," who made their living by waving night sticks, and who ran around keeping one another informed of things; visibly pleased with themselves, those literary ruffians and bureaucrats who excelled in "trimming their sails" predicted that there would be another anti-rightist campaign. This indeed made people shudder.

I very much wonder why the exposure of crimes on the part of the Gang of Four, depicting their corruption and shady dealings in stories and plays, would cause such a group of "gentlemen" to be so indignant, as though their ancestral graves had been violated. Were these high priests of morality defending brightness or darkness?

Now many comrades are worried that they may be attacked once again, and have, one after another, asked for the introduction of legislation. This is not without foundation, because a group of people whose profession it is to attack people actually does exist. They appear to be just, but during the past several decades they "injured the people's teeth and eyes while being opposed to retaliation" and were never without their "consistently correct" microscopic glasses with which they searched out "rightist bacteria." If the Party Central Committee had not been wise, these people would have utilized their power to have "all their sons qualified for government posts" in literature and the arts.

I do not wish to be an alarmist, but I do want to use this opportunity to cry out: Our Party, our nation, our people, and the cause
of literature and the arts, simply cannot endure another torrent
of attacks!

Excluding minor ones, we have had three major campaigns since
the founding of the nation: in 1957, 1959, and the Cultural Revolution. In 1957, a large group of writers and artists who were talented, who dared to think and dared to speak, was eliminated. This
group of writers, which comprised a newly emerging force, was
attacked so viciously that they were afraid to speak to one another
when they met. In 1959, another group of good cadres who dared to
speak the truth was eliminated, as was Party democracy, resulting
in a false "communism" woven with lies and causing an unprecedented disaster. After 1962, considerable efforts were made to adjust various policies, thereby providing us with a brief respite.
Then came the Cultural Revolution in 1966, and a decade of catastrophe nearly brought our Party and our country to the point of
extinction.

There are several attitudes to cope with being attacked: some
become hardened, some soften up, some become crafty, and some
simply become confused.

A fact that I do not understand is that some comrades who suffered considerably under Lin Biao, Jiang Qing, and the like and
who, like me, were put into prison, emerged from prison only to
attack others, as though having once been attacked themselves they
were now different from all others and were protected by an im-
pregnable shield and a holier-than-thou attitude. I merely wish to
remind such comrades that the people and comrades in the field of
literature and the arts have traveled everywhere and have appealed
to every quarter in support of your rehabilitation and return to
leadership positions in literature and the arts, with enthusiasm,
sincerity, and hope. Since you have had experience in attacking
others and know what it is like to be attacked by others, you have
been subjected to both positive and negative experiences and lessons. We trust that you will unite the literary and artistic circles
so that we will all dedicate our remaining years to the work of the
Four Modernizations.

Last spring, at the Expanded Session of the All-China Federation
of Literature and Art Circles, Comrade Zhou Yang spoke of
his personal experiences, saying that because he had been attacked
by others he finally knew how it felt. He earnestly and somberly

said, "I have been working in literary and artistic circles for a long time, accumulating a great many debts to others, which I could not pay in full because I was attacked by the Gang of Four." We were deeply moved by his self-analysis and self-correcting attitude, and we hope that all those comrades who were responsible for leading the field of literature and the arts during the past seventeen years will learn from his spirit. Otherwise, every writer and artist would be like "a bird that starts at the sight of a bow" and would be preparing at all times against attacks; in which case, how could anyone talk about the flourishing of creativity?

What I have just said is decidedly not for myself, since I am, for good or for bad, a man in his sixties who could at most spend another four or five years in prison. After the fall of the Gang of Four, and while a group of trailblazers was rushing forward, there emerged a new atmosphere in the movement to liberate thought in literary and artistic circles; now that a few new buds have appeared following the implementation of "let a hundred flowers bloom and a hundred schools of thought contend," by no means let them wither from cold winds.

But I firmly believe that our Party has become more mature than ever before. Documents such as the Summary, which strangle literature and the arts, could not possibly reappear. It will no longer be so easy for anyone to use his own power and influence to strangle literary or artistic individuality or to cut down the banner of realism. As I am aware, many comrades present here have steeled their hearts for the country, for the people, for the socialist cause, and for a movement to emancipate thought that will not be abandoned halfway; for them there is no path but that of a sustained struggle. We must struggle in order that our own misfortune will not be passed on to later generations; we must do so in order that the throats of future Zhang Zhixins will not be slit; we must do so in order that the ideal of the Four Modernizations will not be turned into a mere visionary fancy and that the people will not be fooled again by "seasonal communism"; we must do so in order that our offspring will never become captives of any religion and will be rescued by science. For all of this, what is there for one to fear, even if it should be a steel knife, let alone a label or a stick? It will merely add a new wound upon an old one. Now that the Party and the people have bestowed upon us fighting pens, we must fight and we must dedicate ourselves to the cause of the Party's literature. In the name of the flourishing of our motherland's literature and the arts we fear nothing, even if it means imprisonment for another five or ten years or being burdened with a thousand or ten thousand labels, however filthy they may be; even having our throats cut or being marched to the execution ground does not faze us, for we shall die with no regrets.

III

What we have convened is a Congress of Chinese Writers and Artists. Such a congress has not been called for nineteen years. Since it is a gathering of literary and artistic workers, we would like to have all writers and artists throughout the nation make known some of their wishes and resolve some of their issues. Naturally, there will be some issues that writers and artists will not be able to resolve and that need to be submitted to the Party Central Committee and government units for resolution.

What I have thought of are the following issues:

1. THE ISSUE REGARDING THE "DOUBLE HUNDRED" POLICY

"Let a hundred flowers bloom and a hundred schools of thought contend" was proposed by Chairman Mao twenty-three years ago. [The "Double Hundred" policy] is the only policy that can make the causes of literature, art, science, and culture flourish. This subject has been discussed at all meetings over the past twenty-some years, whatever the makeup of our leadership. The bitter experience in literary and artistic circles during these years, however, has been the greatest irony where the "Double Hundred" policy is concerned. As I think back carefully, I see that a ridiculous situation developed following the proposal of the "Double Hundred" policy. While the slogan of "let a hundred flowers bloom and a hundred schools of thought contend" was being shouted, complaints created by countless literary inquisitions were heard everywhere. In the movement to emancipate thought after the fall of the Gang of Four, practice has emerged as the sole criterion for determining truth. Should we or should we not use our practice of the past twenty-some years to verify the six criteria that were superimposed on the "Double Hundred" policy? If these criteria are not clarified and given complete and totally correct explanations, the "Double Hundred" policy will be nothing but empty talk.

We must have a fair and just evaluation of our literary and artistic creative team. I believe that an absolute majority of writers ardently love the Party and socialism. It may also be said that since an absolute majority of writers were cultivated by the Party, what reasons would they have to oppose the Party and socialism, to which they had dedicated themselves? But since the anti-rightist campaign, a strange phenomenon has appeared: In the eyes of the leaders at various levels, all those who wield pens seem to be dangerous characters who are to be considered "rightists." Yet those who write happen to be gossipy, sensitive, and imaginative — if they were not imaginative, they would not be writers — and consequently are often in conflict with senior officials at various levels and inevitably bear the brunt of the attacks. Major writers are subjected to major attacks; minor writers are subjected to minor attacks. A club labeled anti-Party and anti-socialism is seemingly forever suspended over their heads. What can be done about this? The power of explanation with regard to the "Double Hundred" policy rests in the hands of senior officials at all levels!

I believe that the "Double Hundred" policy must be established as a Constitution of Literature and the Arts. The Eight Principles for Literature and the Arts were prescribed in 1962. Now there is an even stronger need to make a few more provisions. These provisions ought to be even more thought-emancipating and more explicit than the Eight Principles. I believe that they should especially address the following: All persons with rights of citizenship shall have the right to publish their works, which, apart from editing, shall not be subject to any censorship. Censorship of this kind shall be deemed illegal....

2. THE ISSUE REGARDING LAWS
RELATING TO PUBLICATION

At the Second Session of the Fifth People's Congress I introduced a proposal: to establish laws relating to publishing. The Proposal-Examining Committee responded with its comments very forthrightly: "Refer to the Bureau of Publications for disposition." I do not know what has happened to this proposal, but I wish that the Bureau of Publications would attach some importance to this issue.

Here I would like to say a few more words.

At the present time, we do not have any law governing writing and publication. There are no copyrights nor rights of publication. If

there were, they would apply only when one's work was being criticized, and, even if it was unpublished, it would be fished out of a
suitcase and punishment would be fixed accordingly. Liu Zhidan,
a novel, was criticized as being a major anti-Party poisonous weed
before the readers even saw it. It further implicated more than ten
thousand people. One cannot but be indignant over such a case.

If there are no copyrights or rights of publication, the statement
that one must be responsible for one's own writing is idle talk.

Our Constitution stipulates that citizens enjoy freedom of speech
and freedom of press. Laws relating to publications are legal instruments to safeguard such freedoms and rights. They also include the author's economic rights. I am not advocating economism,
but I do regard these rights as concerns of young writers that the
Chinese Writers Association ought to consider. At present, an author's remuneration is something one feels coy about, something
that is neither fish nor fowl. Even by spending money, one might
not be able to purchase good works. Yet if the author should sub-
sidize it, he still might not be able to publish an important work....
I suggest that we raise remunerations for authors and institute the
practice of royalties. Whether or not a novel is well received by
the readers should definitely be the major criterion in evaluating
it. If it should sell many copies, the remuneration should be greater. In so doing, we would not only have given expression to such an
important criterion, but would also have given encouragement to
socialist competition in creative work.

Frankly speaking, I have often thought that, after a period of time,
creative writing ought to become a free profession, with no wages,
so that writers are free from blackmail from superiors. At present,
Comrade Ba Jin is probably the only person in the whole country
who does not receive wages! I have not received wages for several
years, but it does not work for me, for I began to borrow within
five years. But I think that if we really want creative works to
flourish, after we have done what has to be done with matters concerning copyrights and royalties, and the work of the Writers Association, authors will necessarily follow this route. It will save a
great deal of trouble: it may save one from being jabbed and
prodded from behind and from being charged with moonlighting; it
may also prevent the leadership from whispering accusations that
we are hard to lead. At the present time, there are indeed things
that are unreasonable. Some people are nominally given the name
of writer, but do no creative writing, yet receive wages neverthe-

CHEN DENGKE: SUGGESTIONS FOR LITERARY WORK   101

less. In reality, writers' creative works originate from a sense of social responsibility. Authors cannot be appointed by imperial decree, nor can they be self-appointed. If they do not produce works, no matter how elegantly their Writers Association membership cards are printed, they are of no use. Only those whose works are used by society and whose impact has established credibility with the people may be considered writers. They are part and parcel with society.

Our present procedures for managing authors and creative works truly deserve further study.

3. THE ISSUE CONCERNING DEMOCRATIC AND LEGAL SYSTEMS

During the past two years many comrades have dealt with the issue [concerning democratic and legal systems]. I mention it again because I feel that, since we are such a large country, we ought to have a few legal provisions to safeguard the inalienable rights of authors and artists of creative freedom and of life.

I have another novel idea: should the All-China Federation of Literary and Art Circles and the various Writers Associations have a legal counsel? If the Writers Association does not have such an authorized post, we would be willing to use our membership dues to engage counsel. If, at a later time, an issue should arise, it would be straightforwardly dealt with in accordance with the provisions of law. If it should be an issue of ideology, it would be dealt with as such; if it should be a political issue, it would be dealt with as such. The reasonable divergence of views, as seen in the period when "a hundred schools of thought were contending with one another," ought to be actively promoted. Those who lodge false accusations against a work or an author should be legally indicted. Otherwise, since men of letters can do nothing but carry on their fights on paper, a few years from now it would still be idle talk. One word from those with power and influence would be fatal to an author. Historical tragedies of the past cannot be reenacted.

Let me have one final word. The All-China Federation of Literary and Art Circles, be definition, is a mass organization of writers and artists. It should and must elect its leadership structure through democratic means. We must trust that, having undergone several decades of discipline, representatives of literary and artistic circles have greatly elevated their consciousness, and, based on their several decades of practice in struggles between two lines, they know how to judge people.

Translated by Maurice H. Tseng
(Kaipi shehuizhuyi wenyi fanrong de xin shiqi)

10

THE CALL OF THE TIMES

Liu Binyan

1. TAKING ORDERS FROM THE PEOPLE

Among the middle-aged delegates at our meeting today, some — Bai Hua, Wang Meng, Deng Youmei, Shao Yanxiang, Cong Weixi, Gong Liu, Liu Shaotang — have shown themselves to be the most lively and spectacular writers of prose and poetry on the literary stage over the last two or three years. But without a single exception, they are all the "rightists" of 1957. They should not look as old as they do today. Sometimes I comfort myself by thinking that the losses we suffered were not, in the final analysis, ours alone. If during the last twenty years we had been allowed to write a bit, if comrades who died had not died — Comrade Fan Zheng from the Northeast, for example, who at twelve was a revolutionary and at fourteen joined the Party, and who authored the story "Xia Hongqiu" and the play Ji Hongchang — comrades like that, who were far greater writers than I, had not died, even if they had only produced one play or one novel each year, what would our literary history look like now? It is a painful thought. Suppose we did make mistakes; didn't we have the right to make them? Why is it that scientists and politicians can make mistakes but writers and artists alone may not? If scientists are forgiven their mistakes because they have no social effect, what about politicians? Surely an essay of a couple of pages or a dozen pages cannot cause greater harm than the mistakes made by politicians. Why must these comrades be deprived of the right to live and the right to create? When it comes to the right to make mistakes, I think all men should be equal.

I am ashamed to say that, compared to the comrades mentioned above, I am the weakest, for in 1962 I washed my hands of everything. To use the Japanese expression, I "abandoned the fight." I

cut myself off from Chinese literature because I could see no future
in it. I cannot therefore be compared to the others; I am exceptionally weak. It is as though my heart were a void. But today we
cannot feel satisfied with this response; we cannot help thinking of
those who have been implicated with us for twenty-two years. Just
because they read our works and said they were good, many readers
still in their teens or twenties were labeled rightists. Some have
not been rehabilitated to this day. Even a character in one of my
stories, the young engineer in "On the Bridge Site," Zeng Gang (his
real name is Zeng Yagang) is still, I recently learned, labeled a
rightist. What crime did he commit? It was not he who spoke out
about problems in the construction of the Yellow River Bridge at
Lanzhou. I sought him out and he told me about his own work; that
is all he did, but he was labeled a rightist.

In my own experience, there was one period I shall never forget:
in the three years from 1958 to 1960, I immersed myself totally in
the life of the people. I slept in the same bed with poor peasants
and even shared their quilt. I devoutly wished to reform myself,
to be reborn. That was my resolve as I set off, but I could not help
pondering the questions: What is the purpose of literature? and
What is the responsibility of the author in our socialist society?
Did everything change on the morning our Party took power? The
laws of literature, its mission and purpose, the responsibility of
the author — had they all changed? I wanted to believe the criticisms in the newspaper, believe that they were justified, so that I
could be content.

As it happened, they were three years of great social change. I
saw the actual situation in the countryside and listened to the peasants as they complained to me of their bitterness. It was exactly
the opposite of what higher levels were saying and the newspapers
were publishing. Why? Whom was I to believe? Whose side
should I take? For three years, my diary was filled with this sort
of thing; I tried with all my heart to turn my thinking around, to
criticize my class attitude and my right-wing views. Even in 1960,
when people had the proof of what was true, I still tried to cast off
the truths that had come to me from the masses and from practice;
I continued to believe the mistaken view passed down by my superiors and the newspapers. Next to Zhang Zhixin, I was nothing. I
had a notebook full of statistics: increases in our nation's grain
production, increases in livestock and increases in steel production
since 1958. I sincerely believed it all. I believed what the Party

said and acted on it, for I wanted to be an obedient tool, to be born again as a new man. I put a great deal of effort into this. I was ready to believe that we could put up higher and higher satellites without end. I was ready to believe that it was right to do without work points and private plots and to communalize the peasants' savings. I was willing to support the free meal system — otherwise, what would happen to the grain surplus? But what could I do when mounds of facts lay before my eyes?

After all, objective material conditions have more strength and power than our subjective will. Even if my commitment to reform myself had been greater, it could not have prevented the barrage of real contradictions in my head.

We were told to set up a zoo in a poor mountain village. At once we were moving earth and digging caves, day and night, for the benefit of lions and tigers. In this village a peasant ate only a few ounces of meat a year, so I asked those in charge if they knew what lions and tigers ate. They don't like maize flour; they like meat.

Since there was no source of water in the village, people and animals relied solely on rainwater. A pool had been dug in the village (later it was lined in stone) so that when it rained water flowed into the pool. Once the water had settled, it was ready to drink. But we were told to build a fountain in the village. Then we had to make a Summer Palace in the hills, destroying acres of farmland, since it was said that we only needed a third of our arable land. Any man with a head on his shoulders who was confronted with one such instance after another was bound to start thinking.

Following that autumn there was a big meeting to celebrate the founding of the commune, complete with drums and gongs. Every commune member was given a little red packet. When the members got them home and opened them they found — one dollar. This was their entire monetary reward for a whole year's work. Under the old plan, the work points for a single day were worth more than a dollar and as much as a dollar and a half. I saw that the peasants wanted one thing, the leadership and newspapers something else, as though the world contained two different truths at the same time. My feelings were in turmoil; it was truly painful. Only in autumn 1960, when the Party Central Committee sent down its "Twelve Points" on rural policy, did the full truth come out and I finally understood. When two things are contradictory, we should listen to the people; we owe our allegiance to the welfare and needs of the people, for they represent the future course of history. Anything

else, no matter how high its authority, that ignores the demands of
the people will never last.

This year we have seen the short stories "A Story Badly Edited"
by Comrade Ru Zhijuan and Comrade Liu Zhen's "Black Flag";
what they describe happened in just that period. It was twenty years
ago, so maybe we should call them historical stories, but when we
read them we find them extraordinarily relevant and moving, as
though they were happening before our very eyes. We should consider what might have happened if these two stories had been published not in 1979 but in 1958. If our people had read such stories
then, could they have turned against the Communist Party? Could
they have overthrown the socialist system? They could not have.
In fact, quite the reverse — this sort of writing would have helped
the Party realize and correct our mistakes earlier. It would have
increased the authority of the Party; at the very least, it could not
have diminished it. It would have made socialist agriculture and
collective economics even more secure, with an even brighter prospect for development. It would have increased the peasants' enthusiasm for both production and politics. Isn't this precisely what
the history of those years has taught us?

History has proved that what really destroys the good name of
the Party and socialism is not this sort of literary creation, which
intervenes in life and reflects real social contradictions, but rather
our mistakes, upon which enemies build and expand through sabo-
tage. This is what has hurt the Party and harmed socialism, tar-
nishing their good name. Isn't this true? But even in 1979, when
these pieces were published, we experienced gratitude for the courage of the editors of People's Literature and Shanghai Literature
and Arts. We must sum up the lessons of experience.

From these three years of my life, I have grasped a truth: we
authors must confront life, we must listen to what the people have
to say, and we must take our orders from the people. Party policy
too must undergo the test of practice. What is the test of practice?
The test of practice is the test of the people. Aren't the people the
masters of practice? Can't Party policy also be mistaken? The
Party is not infallible. If things are wrong they should be put right.
Anyone who really cares for the Party will surely not object to correcting its mistakes. When the sort of double truth I mentioned
above appears in our lives, writers should obey their feeling of
great responsibility to the people to present their conclusions, not
hastily but responsibly, not as supporting singers but through inde-

pendent thought. Hasn't practice shown that many of the works describing village life during this period that were published at the time are now lifeless? I believe that the stories by Liu Zhen and Ru Zhijuan will, in contrast, have a long life.

Secondly, in the minds of some comrades, there seems to be the notion that if literature intervenes in life, then it is concerned with only the dark side, as though progressive characters and heroic figures were excluded. This is a misunderstanding. Do we not see in the stories of Ru Zhijuan and Liu Zhen exceptionally good and moving images of progressive and heroic characters? They emerge among contradictions and develop among contradictions.

Thirdly, literature is a mirror. If what this mirror reflects is not always beautiful, does not always give pleasure, or does not make people happy, I ask the comrades in authority not to blame the mirror, but to look into it and to think up ways of removing from life whatever is not beautiful or what makes people unhappy. Haven't the last twenty years provided proof that, when literature is forbidden to intervene in life, when writers are deprived of the right to reflect the problems of real life, harm is done not only to literature and to the people, but to our Party? Now this period of literary history seems to have come to an end, but it is not completely finished. This is the first issue I want to discuss.

2. ANSWERING THE PEOPLE'S QUESTIONS

Nowadays, disagreements over literary issues are inevitably bound up with people's disagreements on political issues, while these political disagreements are in turn inseparable from the analysis of our society. Some comrades have genuine disagreements with us on how we should analyze our society and our reality. Some, for instance, think that Lin Biao and the Gang of Four did not cause much damage, and some even believe that there never was any ultra-left line. Others think that the disasters and poison of that criminal line have already been destroyed and obliterated along with the Gang of Four; now it is a question of looking ahead, with everyone working together.

My view is that the full extent of the disasters caused by Lin Biao and the Gang of Four has not yet been disclosed and that people have not yet fully realized the significance of what has been exposed. We should not think of this baneful influence as something lifeless and motionless, obediently waiting for us to clear it out; it is a living social force, a force with a social base.

This May, I personally got a dose of this baneful influence. I was invited to a provincial meeting of young writers to give a talk. During the talk I happened to cite an example and criticize a slogan. Suddenly I was in deep trouble. What had I done wrong? I had "attacked a certain large enterprise." Was my example true? It was. Was there any problem with the slogan I criticized: "Work your hardest for eight hours, then do some more out of the goodness of your heart"? It certainly is worthy of discussion. But no, so-and-so doesn't present his side or debate the issue; he goes off to report the crime to three provincial Party secretaries, and the matter is blown all out of proportion. Times had changed, however, even though it was May and there was still a chill wind blowing against the Third Plenum; many comrades stood up, spoke out for justice, defended and encouraged me. As a result, I wound up with several new friends. I learned three things from this incident: First, even if their number is small (it could not have been more than two percent in an audience of over four hundred), in the right political climate these people can become a political force to be reckoned with. Second, there still exists in China the strange phenomenon that good cannot triumph over evil; a speaker may remove every mention of "letting a hundred flowers bloom, a hundred schools of thought contend" and the democratization of literature and art from his talk, and not only does he do so at no personal risk, he can even present himself as "holding high the banner." If, however, one promotes the emancipation of thought adopted by the Third Plenum, one cannot escape accusations. Third, times have indeed changed; gone forever is the scene where the "leftists" had only to give the order for everyone to rush up and attack someone. This is no small development in Chinese political history.

What should concern us most are the invisible disasters. The Gang of Four destroyed our Party's body, destroyed our connection to society. They turned the relationship between Party and masses into an abnormal one. The problem was that some people, although they were not themselves bad, actively supported wrongdoers. They looked like Party members or Party cadres. Alive and active, always with a vested interest and their own ideology, they were bound to serve this function. Without decisive measures and determined fighting, it will be difficult to turn this situation around.

We must not, under any circumstances, describe the ultra-Left line, which Lin Biao and the Gang of Four pursued for a decade, as

merely a deviation, dismissing it as the sort of disaster that can
be wiped out by criticism alone. The roots of ultra-leftism go deep
in our society. Think back to the "Left" opportunist line of Wang
Ming; didn't the Party launch a large-scale campaign of criticism?
In addition to ideological criticism, there was also an organizational
rectification. However, even though the correct line of Comrade
Mao Zedong held the leading position in the Party from the late thirties, the "leftist" deviation in our daily life and practical work was
never completely destroyed and was able to cause great damage.
The rectification movement started out opposing the "Left," and
later became a "leftist" deviation. Land reform, the policy toward
urban industry and commerce in the War of Liberation, and the policy on intellectuals were all to varying degrees "leftist" deviations,
which held sway on a large scale. When we brought land reform to
the countryside around Harbin early in 1947, Comrade Jiang Nan-
xiang was our leader. Time and again he warned each work team
that there was to be no physical punishment of landlords. But our
group was no sooner in a village than we strung up a minor land-
lord, cruelly tortured him, and accused him of hiding weapons and
valuables. He was beaten every evening until the flesh showed
through his broken skin. The result: he had nothing; we dug up only
a few pieces of battered cotton quilting. This shows that even if the
leadership has not suggested it, even when it emphatically opposes
it, ultra-left action can appear spontaneously and cannot be prevented from bursting forth.

When Marx and Engels wrote about England and Germany, they
considered not only their strong points but also the weaknesses in
national character. Lenin often spoke of the persistence of the
brand marks of serfdom in Russia. Ours is a great nation, outstanding in diligence, courage, and genius. But several thousand
years of feudal rule and the fact that even now we have not broken
with the pattern of small-scale production make it impossible for
our national character not to have retained the brand marks of feudalism, especially the characteristics of the small-time peasant and
petty bourgeoisie, and feudal ways of thinking. Compared to the
peasant class of Western Europe, our peasants are much more revolutionary. In the National Democratic Revolution, under the leadership of the Party, China's peasants kept up a difficult and arduous struggle over a long period. But since the peasants are a class
without a future, since the peasant class faced destruction whether
capitalism or socialism was victorious, and because of the limita-

tions of their production methods (production divided year after year, always small-scale and simple), it is a comparatively conservative class, prone to fantasy. Its highest aim is egalitarianism; the means of reaching its ideal is inevitably anarchism. The small-scale peasant economy requires no progress in science or culture, even to the point where it is hostile to science and culture and their representative — the intellectual. Marx said that man's ability to understand the world with cool detachment only developed in the capitalist period. If the capitalist class had not found ways to make the highest profits, it would not have survived the competition; acting according to objective laws was a necessity (except when these laws imperiled the existence of the whole capitalist class). The petty bourgeoisie was not like this; Marx, Engels, and Lenin often described the reactionary nature of petty bourgeois thinking.

In our country, generally speaking, the social base of the ultra-left line is this great ocean of small-scale farmers. That is why Comrade Mao Zedong said: "A critical problem is the education of the peasants." Basically, now and in the foreseeable future, the main cause of upheaval in China is the ultra-left ideology, with its element of anarchism, which derives from this social base. If we look back over our history since Liberation, what has caused the greatest calamities, bourgeois thinking or a combination of petty bourgeois and feudal attitudes? This question deserves consideration. Does the poverty and backwardness of our land make it easier for rightist opportunism to grow? Or does it encourage leftist opportunism? In their analysis of leftist opportunism in the workers' movements in England and Germany, Marx and Engels suggested two reasons for the tendency: on one side there was a strong, wealthy, and experienced bourgeoisie; on the other, a strong working class. The latter achieved a certain degree of democratic rights, gained daily experience of struggle, and became a huge force that threatened the bourgeoisie. At this the bourgeoisie did not hesitate to use their super-profits to buy out, corrupt, and undermine the working class (at first it was only a part, the "workers' aristocracy"), and so rightist opportunism appeared in the communist movement.

In China, the situation was very different; at any rate, China had a comparatively weak and penniless bourgeoisie and did not have a strong working class with democratic rights. Since Liberation, the whole nation, including the peasantry, has always been wholehearted and enthusiastic in the desire to transform our "poor and blank" country as soon as possible; unfortunately, the practice arose of overlooking objective limitations and ignoring objective laws. It was always "oppose the Right and never the 'Left'"; the catastrophes, unprecedented in human history, caused by Lin Biao and the Gang of Four, with their ultra-left line, nearly destroyed Party and country, and we still have not fully recovered. But "Left" is still not a dirty word and practitioners of "leftism" can still swagger about and earn publicity — they run no risks. Meanwhile, people who cling to Marxism and who support the correct policy direction of the Third Plenum of the Party have to be wary and uneasy, always worried about being beaten or being "capped." Doesn't the persistence of this strange phenomenon show how secure the roots of "leftism" are and how "leftism" is far more dangerous than the Right? Here I want to alert you, comrades, to the fact that the ultra-left, always active though unseen in our midst, is the main obstacle to the achievement of the Four Modernizations; it is the main cause of political disturbance. We must not ascribe the main cause of unrest to what the Left has created or influenced (such as the reasonable requests of those who suffered injustice) and then let the leftists themselves get off scot-free.

Some comrades think that the main task of literature is to describe heroic figures (or progressive characters), what we call "eulogizing"; in other words, singing the virtues of heroic figures. I would like to describe a few situations for them to ponder over. In the particular historical conditions that exist today, we find a peculiar phenomenon, unseen in the fifties and sixties. Our heroes are never very secure now. In the fifties, I worked for a newspaper and I know that writing critical reports for the papers was not an easy job. Of course it was not as difficult as it is today, even though, in general, critical reports are better now. What is this strange phenomenon? I was told in Heilongjiang that not only are critical reports tricky, but even singing praises is difficult. It is hard for a newspaper to print things about good people. If good people are doing good works, someone will be offended. If one writes admiringly of good people it means that one is attacking bad people, at any rate people who are not very good. So it is the good people who are in trouble. They say that if you want to trap someone, eulogize him in the newspaper. There are many such examples: praise a man long and often enough and he will end up discredited for sure. If you think about it, who does not have faults? But what these people do is add a few imaginary faults to your real ones, spread it around, and then use the power they have to reprimand and make life difficult for you; in the end you have a hard time of it.

There was a young policewoman called Liu Jie, from Anling District in Daxing, who was favorably presented in the Heilongjiang Daily. Since 1975, this comrade had upheld the principles of the Party and was impartial in administering the law. When her station chief told her to give someone a residence permit and she found on investigation that he was not really related to any local person, she refused. She stood by her decision. What was the result? After the Heilongjiang newspapers had held her up as a model, her station chief, police chief, and district leaders got together to attack her. She had been an activist for the Party and wanted to join, but now her application was denied. Although she had been a progressive in the public security system, this was no longer acknowledged. There was even an attempt on her life, but the assailant was never caught. In contrast, the police chief lost his dog and it was found the next day — but a homicidal criminal to this day has not been apprehended. The local reporter who wrote the story is also under attack. So I say to those comrades who advocate the description of progressive and heroic characters, who think that intervening in life excludes the portrayal of progressive characters, to go out and see for themselves how our heroes are faring these days.

There are writers and critics who say that our literature should support the Four Modernizations, which they interpret as writing about production or the development of science and technology. I would like to ask them to consider the situation. What is our production like now? Doesn't writing about production mean writing about people and their level of enthusiasm? What is the state of our people's enthusiasm? Some of our factories have a sort of feudal, patriarchal management. The workers have no democratic rights and the manager can promote according to his personal preference. If workers are a little impertinent, they will meet with vindictive retaliation. In Heilongjiang I once made a special investigation to determine what was preventing the working masses from being more enthusiastic about their work. Of course, the reinstatement of the labor incentive principle of "to each according to his work" was an important factor, and it took a lot of fighting for. But did this "to each according to his work" or "the more you work the more you get" produce enthusiasm among the workers? It is now quite clear that this was not enough. Money alone cannot buy enthusiasm. Some people win a prize that equals or exceeds their income, yet there is no guarantee of their working hard. This is a truth that Chairman Mao spoke of; in "Notes on Political Economy" he said that, if a factory's management was bureaucratic, workers would not consider the factory their own, but would think of it as the leadership's. That's the position we are in now.

When we went to the Binxian Towel Factory to talk to six old workers, two people nearby were eavesdropping, with the Head of Personnel taking the lead. Three days after we left, one after another of the men was victimized, not one of them being lucky enough to escape. That is how things stand. Some of our workers today still lack an attitude of personal independence. We should consider our personnel system; people neither move freely nor choose their work; if you offend your boss, he can "give you small shoes," and you have no way of exposing or fighting him. What do you do? You have to put up with his temper all your life. If you are bullied but persist in your view, your family gets hurt too. A man is, after all, a human being — he needs some respect, he needs some freedom, he needs care and consideration. As it happens, those are precisely what we lack today. What he needs above all is fairness, for a sense of morality and justice is one of man's distinguishing attributes. He demands justice. Even if an injustice does him no harm personally, it leaves a scar in his heart and he is unhappy. Can you expect a man who is unhappy, a man who goes to work with a frown and who is worried about his daily needs to labor with all his heart and strength, to be concerned with national and international affairs? "Work your hardest for eight hours, then do some more out of the goodness of your heart"; even if you think of a man as a production tool, he is still a living tool and needs to replenish his strength. He also has his family life, a need to rest and study, and he requires a bit of cultural activity. If we see man as a tool and not as the revered object of our service, then we are wrong. What does The Manifesto of the Communist Party say? Does it not say that for the ideal society "the free development of each is the condition for the free development of all," and call for man's total development? Surely we do not want to keep postponing human development until tomorrow, anticipating a day when a sudden explosion brings forth a perfect, fully developed man? Shouldn't we start today on the gradual perfection of our people? Marx said that for a man to be a true man he needs an environment suited to his nature. Then shouldn't we create this environment?

When we write about the Four Modernizations, therefore, we

must not avoid writing about what stands in their way or what prevents our workers from being enthusiastic, things that crush them so that they cannot hold up their heads. Would a real progressive close his eyes before such a state of affairs? Of course, there probably are some true model workers, but can it really be enough for a model worker who is deserving of the name progressive to break a few production records? Every age has its own heroes. Why did "Manager Qiao Assumes Office" receive such a welcome? The protagonist is the hero of our time, the spirit of our time. When we are describing a worker of today, even if he is just an ordinary worker, he should not close his eyes to the problems of our time, as if completely ignorant. If we did that we would be encouraging stupidity and ignorance and would be encouraging people to be apathetic and unconcerned about the Party and socialism. We do not need many heroes of that sort. Ignorance is terrifying. I learned that much on my trip to the Northeast. When someone opposed the line of the Third Plenum or was suspicious of it, it was not because he had a vested interest to protect or because it violated some entrenched traditional attitude, but rather because of his ignorance. So I began to realize why the ultra-left line of the Gang of Four needed to encourage ignorance among the masses. I also understood the meaning of something said by Chi Qin, which, unfortunately, few people quote: "We must resolutely oppose and prevent revisionism, even if it means reverting back to a primitive communist society." Why does a primitive communist society sound so attractive? Is it because the word communist is so pleasant? Primitive communist society was the period when man had just crossed over from being an animal; life was hazardous every day — it was a society when huge numbers died like animals of cold and hunger. Since the forces of production were so extremely low, people lived an animal-like existence and even practiced cannibalism! Absolute ignorance was the partner of an absolute low in production. And so I understood that the Gang of Four's opposition to revisionism was itself revisionist. If their "revisionism" had not dragged us back but propelled us forward, would we have called it revisionism? But if your "revolution," your "Marxism," your "socialism" brings us back to primitive communism, then I am sorry, but we had better keep our distance from you. In fact, they had already done this to a certain extent. There are places in China where the extent of poverty and ignorance is in strong contrast to our socialist system. Thirty years! We must think about them, comrades!

I said just now that literature should answer the people's questions. The first question posed by the people — the very same question raised by Comrade Hua Guofeng in his report — is this: given our socialist system and the work our people have done, we have not achieved as much in these thirty years as we should have. This is an important factor in our remaining so poor and underdeveloped. Isn't that so? The people ask another question: if a mistake is made, why is it not corrected? Why is it repeated? The repetition of mistakes is a peculiarity of our age. It seems to me that one important reason for this is that even today we still do not have a scientific understanding of our society that agrees with reality. I think this is most dangerous. I said before that the source of our disagreements lies in our different analyses of society. Does there exist a truly reliable investigation and analysis of the various aspects of our society? No. Such an investigation, a process for understanding our society, has been impossible for more than twenty years. We have entrusted the work of investigating our society to our top leadership comrades. The whole nation, including social scientists and philosophers, is waiting; we are all waiting for a direction; then we will expound upon it. Literature can provide illustrations of this direction. Isn't that precisely how things stand now?

However, in the past, man's knowledge of his condition came about through the efforts of all mankind. There was never a society where the task of analyzing the world or society was entrusted to a small minority. Haven't we writers abandoned the task of analysis? What do we know? What is there that needs our exploration? What is there that will allow our exploration? If it is not done through independent thought we do not want it, and if that's a crime, then so is our concern for our country and people. Reality proves that entrusting this work to a few people will not do; even the greatest man would find the task difficult. Lenin said the same thing a long time ago. In his "Materialism and Empirio-Criticism" he said that seventy Marxes would not be able to fully comprehend the world economy at that time. It simply could not be done. The world economy was very simple then, nothing more than a capitalist economy. The situation in one province in China now is much more complex than the world situation in those days. Social development always grows more complex, but our analysis inevitably simplifies it. This is one of the reasons why we have suffered and been tricked. When some incident flares up, we are frightened out of our wits; we imagine the whole country to be in trouble, that the sky is going to fall, so we come to a hasty resolution that has to be revised before long. This can shake the people's confidence in us. They think that our policy is fickle. In the twenties, at Lenin's insistence, the Soviet Union encouraged sociology; Stalin discontinued it. Five or six years later, the Soviet Union reinstated sociology and we were going to do the same; unfortunately, it was abandoned. Now it has been discussed again and is being reinstated. What is the state of sociology in the rest of the world? It is very highly developed in Poland, America, the Soviet Union, and Japan. In some countries even a factory may have its own sociology unit. Everything in the factory is in their hands; from production to the pattern of the masses' lives, their modes of thought, and their spiritual life, it is all in their hands.

We are very unclear about many things, including our most serious problems and the great burdens we carry — this poses a great danger. Why is this so? Because if we do not have an accurate knowledge of our society, when we make decisions we have no reliable information on which to base them. Moreover, people may not even be speaking the same language: when the masses see a problem, they may blame the leadership, saying that they are wrong; when the leadership sees a problem, they may say that the masses are the real problem. In fact, we have a huge, unknown world before our eyes.

Foreigners do more research on our problems than we do ourselves. Britain, America, West Germany, and Japan are always analyzing our bureaucratic problems, analyzing Soviet and Chinese socialism. What produces bureaucrats and bureaucracy? Can they be overcome? In newspapers and periodicals there is a wide investigation, a free investigation. Unfortunately, in our own country we consign discussion to the high shelves, with the result that some incredible things have happened. For example, consider the problem of whether or not, after all these years of class struggle, there are still classes in China. The old exploiting classes do not exist any longer, but have they been replaced by new classes? If there are no classes, are there new exploiting-class elements? On such an important question we have no analysis, no research. Literature has a responsibility to demonstrate to the people this aspect of real life. We have to admit that in the past we have incurred a debt to the people.

3. THE CALL OF THE TIMES

Lastly, I would like to discuss what sort of literature we need in our age. Of course, our people need all sorts of writing. When I saw the northern Kunqu opera Li Huiniang, I experienced great emotional satisfaction. This was not because I learned anything from it or increased my historical knowledge, but because of the wonderful pleasure it gave me. This is what our people want too. Of course, there are great questions that affect the life of the people in every age, and since these are the questions that concern them most, we must not avoid them. I am not saying that everyone should write about internal contradictions, bureaucratism, or the special privileges mentality. No, I do not advocate that. But the people do need more writers to deal with these topics. Spring Flowers and Power and the Law met with a vigorous reception; while the echoing applause could not be termed unprecedented in the history of our spoken drama, it was unusual. Why did the masses derive so much enjoyment from Qin Xianglian, Fighting Guo Ji, Fighting Yan Song, and The Revenge of Dou E ? Because they released their anger! So I maintain that objections to "intervening in life" have already met their rebuttal from real life. If no contemporary writer intervenes in life, the masses will have to turn to ancient works for something that will satisfy their needs; that is why Magistrate Bao has been so busy these past few years.

Some comrades have asked me to talk about my "Between Men and Ghosts." This piece is another example; its reception was far beyond what I expected. Comrade Wang Meng's "A Newcomer to the Organization Department" had a wide welcome and provoked the opposition of many in the fifties, but my piece seems to have caused an even greater stir. The major reaction to our earlier stories came from the cultural and literary worlds, the media, and young people (especially the literate young, at least those who have a liking for literature and art). Looking back on it now, the scope was very limited. The reaction following the publication of "Between Men and Ghosts" seems to span Party, political, economic, legal, and cultural spheres. As for the place where the incident occurred, Binxian in Heilongjiang, there is no need to mention the vibrations it caused. I was surprised, however, when letters from more remote places like Gansu and Inner Mongolia arrived, saying that my piece "had the effect of an earthquake" in those areas. I feel that this illustrates some of the problems. Since time is limited, I will read you one letter written by a worker, a letter I cherish dearly:

When I read your "Between Men and Ghosts" an indescribable force caused me to crush the glass in my hand to pieces. Glass splinters lacerated my palm, but I felt no pain. In fact, it brought a sensation of euphoria.

Your pen wove a net over Binxian, but why stop there? The characters you wrote of are not peculiar to Binxian, are they? To put it bluntly, it is a microcosm of the whole country and describes a force that is obstructing the Four Modernizations, a force whose defeat is urgent.

In study time after work, I read your "Between Men and Ghosts" to the fourteen workers in my section in a mood of great excitement. The listeners included women with their children, busy young people, and tired old workers who had thoughts of nothing but rest. But for more than three hours of reading, not a single one left; in fact, they called more and more people over. That is how much they wanted to listen. I am not just saying this to flatter you, for that would be a waste of time. I was asked by these workers to write and congratulate you. They wanted to express their hope that our comrade Liu Binyan will continue to tell us the truth in the future, for we no longer want to hear any more lies or deceptions. Real life shows us that, come the end of the month, several families have to run around borrowing to make do; if they didn't they would truly have nothing to eat. There is no way we are going to listen to those songs with their phony happiness again. They are just too far removed from our lives. If we only get happy songs how will we ever be able to change the harsh reality that confronts us? Let me say just a few more words. While the people were listening to "Between Men and Ghosts," one of them called over our local Party secretary. As it happened, I was just reading the bit that says "the Communist Party controls everything — except for itself." He snatched the book out of my hand in a rage. Only when he saw the cover did he toss it back to me and walk off in anger. This shows that there are many people who do not like your essay.

What moved me most was the following paragraph, which I think should encourage us all:

And so, we insignificant workers earnestly hope that you will not be deterred by anonymous letters of warning nor by people who may be waiting for the chance to take their vindictive revenge. Remember that we are behind you; we do not know you, but if you come to us, we will look after you and protect you, since you sang the song that is in our hearts.

So far I have received no letters attacking the essay, so his concern over anonymous letters was probably unnecessary. Of course, this does not mean that there is no opposition, or, for that matter, fierce opposition. A comrade who wrote from Inner Mongolia mentioned that someone there was saying: "Liu Binyan is committing suicide. Since Liberation there has never been such a poisonous

anti-Party, anti-socialist weed as this piece. Once the next Cultural Revolution comes, on the strength of this essay alone he will
die a more miserable death than [the writer] Deng Tuo!" So some
comrades are concerned for me and some wonder why I did it.
For more than twenty years my whole family, young and old, and
my friends and acquaintances have been implicated, so why do I
continue? The reason is very simple: there is no way back. This
is a recent realization, a truth I never grasped before. Was I not
a devoted and ardent worker up until 1966? But that didn't stop
them from capping me as a "rightist." I kept a diary from 1958 to
1960. I was so naive that I kept the diary in an unlocked office
drawer. When I went home after work, the woman Party member
who sat across from me took the opportunity to copy it out every
evening. One morning in June, after I had shed my "rightist" cap
for just two months (I was "uncapped" in March 1966, and had
passed a pleasant two months), there was a wall poster that declared: "The Rightist Liu Binyan's Plotting Has Not Ceased." In
what way had it "not ceased"? It was, of course, the three years
of mental struggle I had chronicled. I had done my utmost to turn
myself around, had been utterly committed, but it was not enough;
my plotting had not ceased, so what was I to do?

As a matter of fact, the same thing happened to several writers.
Some comrades wrote essays that were full of praise between 1957
and 1966, but once the Cultural Revolution came, they were still
put in cattle sheds and overthrown, weren't they? So there is no
way back for any of us. When I was in the Northeast, comrades
advised me that since there had already been such a commotion, I
should keep my mouth shut. If I kept quiet, people would have no
way of starting rumors or distorting what I said, but if they began
with their wild accusations, I would have no way to explain myself.
I thought it over and decided that I had to speak out. If I didn't,
then what was I doing back in the Party? What would it mean then
to be a communist? What would my life mean?

There is a fable that a crow once said to an eagle: "Because you
eat living flesh and blood, you only live for thirty years; I eat
corpses and may live to be a hundred. Why don't you copy me and
live a few years longer?" The eagle tried to copy him, but after a
day of eating corpses, he said he had had enough: "I would rather
eat living flesh and blood and live only thirty years." The meaning
of the fable is clear. What sort of life is worth living? We have
all experienced life under the Gang of Four! In the morning you

switched on the transistor radio and you heard the same old thing. You opened the newspaper and there it was again; even the headlines weren't worth looking at. You came home after a hard day's work and there wasn't a thing worth reading. When there was a meeting, you couldn't say what you wanted to say and had to say what you didn't want to say. Where was the "life" in such an existence? Surely we don't want our sons and grandsons to go through the same thing! I think it is very simple: there is no way back. If you look at my article on intervening in life in Shanghai Literature and Art, you'll see that there is enough there to call me a rightist. But even if I write a hundred pieces, I can only be labeled a rightist once.

We have mounds of problems and difficulties before us, but the ice is already broken and the ship's course is set; the great ship that is China cannot turn back. There will be complications and obstacles, but we will not repeat those historical mistakes. China's affairs are complex and the time calls for us to fight: full of passion and clear in mind, we must fulfill the sacred mission that the people have bestowed on our nation's literature!

Translated by John Beyer
(Wenyibao, 1979, Nos. 11-12)

11

MAN IS THE AIM, MAN IS THE CENTER

Liu Binyan

I

When we look back over the period that has just ended, we see that the fate of our national literature is bound closely to the fate of the people and the fate of mankind. The harm to the country caused by the ultra-left line of Lin Biao and the Gang of Four was, in the final analysis, done to the people; it was harm to their minds and bodies, to the material and spiritual conditions of their lives, to their advancement and happiness. Of all the destruction, it is the damage to the people's spiritual world, what is called "internal injury," that is the most difficult to repair. Since literature is for people and about people, this damage could not help but injure our literature too.

The injury of the proletariat in the name of the proletariat, the injury of the people in the name of the people, a counterrevolutionary plot in the name of the revolution — we have seen it happen in our individual experience. For a collective experience, just take a look at what fate befell the working masses under "class struggle" and "all-around dictatorship" in one of our "progressive," "Daqing-type" enterprises in Heilongjiang:

Workers at the Huanan Transport Company were up at 4:30 a.m. to begin their "class-struggle"; after hours of "struggle," they started their work. When they came back in the evening, they had to attend a "class struggle meeting" of the whole company for several hours more. Every day it was 4:30 in the morning to 10 at night, with no exception for holidays. Anyone who did not "join battle" was not only criticized himself but his family was punished as well: "No political future" meant no income. Who were the objects of "class struggle"? One worker in leather shoes was criticized as bourgeois; he was said to have been "seized" by the bourgeoisie.

For the sake of a few fish, one worker was attacked for thirty-four days on end. Driver Tang Wenli was sworn at by his boss Zhao Yufeng and answered back; for this he was deprived of his right to drive, had to work under supervision, and was labeled a "production saboteur"; he was actually locked up for three years as an enemy who "hated the Party and socialism." A Party member, Bian Weisi, a model train attendant in the Hejiang District, reported problems in the company to her superiors; she was criticized till she was hovering between life and death. Ill as she was, she was dragged to the company's "line analysis meeting," whose members analyzed her stomach; they said she wasn't a victim of an enlarged liver, but could blame her swollen abdomen on her old man. When her condition became serious she went into the hospital. Not only did she receive no wages, they even sent people to attack her in the hospital, harassing her until blood seeped from her nose and mouth.

A platform inspector, Liu Shulan, was brutally attacked because she would not let the friends of a leading official board a train without a ticket. Several times, to make fun of her diseased womb, Zhao Yufeng forced her to take down her trousers at meetings. When it became serious she went into the hospital, womb and anus swollen together; they sent people to the hospital to drag her back on a truck, without trousers, for more struggle.

When the cashier Zhang Yucai rejected bribes, he was sent off to do manual labor and continually criticized. In the counterattack on the "rightist wind to reverse the verdicts" he was said to be "Deng Xiaoping's social base"; when the Gang of Four was smashed, he was said to be the "teeth and claws of the Gang." All you have to do is disagree with your boss, and even if you have a serious illness you will not be let off. In a "hospital study group" people whose feet had been scalded by boiling water, tuberculosis victims, people with stomach ulcers — they were all lumped together in the political work office. As for Zhao Yufeng, who managed all this "class struggle," he did not regard workers as men. Whenever he spoke to them he swore: "X X your ancestors!" "X X your mother!" "X X your grandmother's grandmother!" This man, who stole public property, who took over houses, and who sought pleasure and profit for himself, was praised by the Party committee above him as a leading figure in "fighting corruption and preventing the evolution of anti-Party activities."

This was obviously not the most terrible type of "class struggle" because no one died. Nor did I mention this case because it shows

how good and bad changed places. I just want everyone to note:
Why is it that masses of workers, including the best, suffered personal insult and injury over a long period of time and still there has
been no justice? Why was the theory of "class struggle," when
there was actually no class enemy, allowed to persist for so long
at the cost of the dignity and health of so many?

When Lin Biao and the Gang of Four were in power, the lack of
democracy and a legal system was of course an important reason.
But before and after they held power were individuals spared from
suffering insult and injury? When a basic precondition of legality
and democracy — respect for the basic rights of all citizens — does
not exist, how can there be true legality and democracy?

One reason why class struggle persisted for so long over such a
wide area without check, why the legal system and democracy were
unsound for so long without anyone's thinking it unusual was that we
still had not gotten rid of our feudal attitudes on man's status and
on personal relations. When people can put up with "not treating
workers as human beings," we have the roots of disaster.

II

Putting a taboo on or censoring the word "human" is unacceptable.
Every concept has its opposite. The popular masses are the opposite category to the ruling class; the proletariat is the opposite
category to the bourgeoisie and all exploiting classes; the poor and
lower-middle peasants are the opposite categories to the landlords,
rich peasants, and wealthy middle peasants. Humans alone are the
opposite category to nature, to gods, to objects, and to animals.

If we avoid the concept "human," how will be deal with the relationship between man and gods. Which is superior, man or gods?
Progressive thinkers throughout history have always had faith in
man's strength, have considered man the greatest; he has relied
upon his continually improving reason and on science to progres-
sively overcome nature; he has used his own ability to solve his
problems without recourse to the help of gods or the supernatural.

> There are a million kinds of spirits in the world
> But not one that is a match for man.

This is a poem from ancient Greece. When the bourgeoisie appeared
on the stage of history, Shakespeare wrote the following in celebra-

tion of man the noble, the great:

> What a piece of work is man! How noble in reason!
> how infinite in faculty! in form, in moving, how
> express and admirable! in action how like an angel!
> in apprehension how like a god! the beauty of the world!
> the paragon of animals!

However, man cannot achieve this state in a capitalist society. Even though he has achieved the production ability we see today, solving man's physical problems of clothing and feeding, this cannot wipe out man's spiritual hunger; hence the spread of emotional crises in the capitalist world. For man to gradually aspire to an ideal world, we need socialism and communism.

It is not, however, a case of sailing with the wind. Feudal thinking, the small-scale peasant mentality, and ultra-left ideology always place a low value on man, separating the individual from the group, man's mind from his body, ideology from feeling. This has caused great damage to our literature.

The ultra-left line separates the individual from the class and nation of which he is part, creating an antithesis; it considers the individual's well-being — his needs, his aspirations, his pleasures, and his contentment — to be incompatible with the well-being of the group; it takes individuality and individualism as synonymous, rejecting and suppressing any sign or development of individuality. Since each man is an independent being, physically and spiritually, his existence must necessarily be that of an autonomous individual. If a class or nation gets rid of the enterprise, the energy, and the individuality of each individual, where will it find the strength to survive? In the feudal socialist kingdom of the Gang of Four, in the name of "revolution," people had to allow their material needs to be kept at the lowest level, just as Chi Qun foresaw — "in order to oppose and prevent revisionism," it was necessary "to revert to primitive communism." If the broad masses were not perfectly content with a life of self-denial, it would not have been possible for that small group to indulge freely in sensual pleasure! Genuine love and friendship and all that is needed to elevate and enrich the mind were forbidden or classed as trivial; otherwise it would not have been possible to implement spiritual egalitarianism without material egalitarianism, and to make the Chinese, with their already low level of science and culture, once again "synonymous with poor and lower-middle peasants," shaving heads throughout 9,600,000 square kilometers in order to disseminate obscurantism!

Like all the religions in history, they separated man's body and soul, asking people to undergo physical suffering to attain spiritual purity and the bliss of some future holy world. Every emotion and desire had to be renounced; the lower the level of life the better. In wartime, the working people were able to put up with hunger and suffer the greatest of sacrifices to ensure the existence of their country and class. But in times of normality and peace, men's bodies have their limits. Excessive labor, the existence of semi-starvation and overcrowded living conditions, make it difficult for men to sustain the lofty ideal of sacrifice for "world revolution."

Ideology and emotion were also separated. It must be that emotion is too much involved with the impure body and its desires, so it does not seem so dependable an ideology. Ideology is abstract, but emotion cannot easily be considered abstract; it is always bound up with the specific well-being and wishes of specific people. This could never be satisfactory to the Gang of Four, but it was beyond their control.

Under this line we produced works that only had abstract class representatives and no specific people or individual traits, characters soaring in spirit but dull in the flesh, with lofty thoughts and empty feelings. Their "heroic characters" and their whole policy of attacking "food and sex are his characteristics" and any other "theory of human nature," ancient or modern, Chinese or foreign, showed to the whole world that man need not eat, need not marry, and is completely without desires; when we achieve a world without human beings, then at last "Gao Daquan"* can become a "heroic figure" who can be applied to any century! The only special thing about such a literary work is that it makes people apathetic, indifferent, and bored.

Of course such heroes have more of the nature of god than of man. But life was different from their literature. Getting rid of human nature meant not the appearance of godly nature but the spread of animal nature. This is hardly surprising; were not Lin Biao, the Gang of Four, and their henchmen themselves the embodiment of animal nature? They spread poverty; the weaker the country became, the greedier and wilder was their desire for money. They promoted ignorance; the more ignorant people became, the more likely they were to endure the control of beasts like tigers and wolves.

While the "model dramas" promoted godliness with a roll of

---

*The proletarian hero in Hao Ran's novel The Golden Highway, one of the few "approved" literary works during the Cultural Revolution. — H. G.

drums and the beating of gongs, a real drama, much more lively and forceful, was being acted out day and night in city and village, showing what animals are like: fascist violence meant brutal attacks, torment, and violent death for the innocent; it meant criminals under the red flag wantonly abusing people's property, their dignity, and their safety. Good and honest men met with misfortune, the bad were always rapidly promoted, chickens and dogs learned to fly ... their godly nature disguised an animal one, trampling and extinguishing human nature without mercy — this is the sort of thing that bunch of criminals did in those ten years.

III

Socialist man should have greater dignity, pride, and perfection than man under the capitalist system. Capitalism freed man from the fetters of feudalism, giving him a measure of freedom, rights, and dignity. This was one central reason why people under capitalism could increase labor productivity to levels several times higher than those in feudal society and create a spiritual civilization. If socialism wants to create a productivity, science, and culture that will surpass capitalism, it must release even greater enthusiasm and initiative from the popular masses: man will then take another step toward his liberation; his social position and mental attitude will truly coincide with his position of master of the People's Republic.

Over the years the taboo on "human" and "human nature" has arisen out of a fear of contamination from the bourgeoisie. In fact the achievements of man under capitalism — in material and cultural affairs and in many other ways — were not the sole property of the bourgeoisie. Even when they were their property — such as their theories of "man" and "human nature" — they are certainly not complete rubbish, nor are they altogether useless and harmful to the proletariat.

Marx placed no taboo on man and his nature. His expositions on the peculiarities of man often derive from bourgeois thinkers. For example, he said of himself: "Whatever pertains to man, I am not a stranger to that." These are the words of the ancient Roman poet Terence; he meant that he was not a god but a man, and thus he had all the attributes that are shared by all men. Hegel also used this Latin proverb; it was certainly not invented by the proletariat. Marx recognized that there was such a thing as human nature and certainly did not think that bourgeois theories on man and human nature should be rejected wholesale.

Why is the mere mention of human nature a denial of man's class nature? Who said that class nature, especially that of the most advanced class in history, the proletariat, could not coexist with human nature? In the most bitter and tense crises of class struggle, a soldier must suppress some of the feelings and instincts he would have in normal life; but is it not his love for the broad masses of people that encourages him to risk death? This love is surely not in contradiction to his sympathy for all degraded and injured people. Furthermore, man is always a man first, the member of a class second; class nature rests on human nature. If there were not some nature common to men, many things in the world could neither be explained nor set in motion.

The original idea behind the taboo on, even the denial of, human nature may have been to protect the interests of the proletariat and prevent losses in the class struggle due to sympathy for the enemy. But, like so many other things, it was pushed beyond reasonable limits and produced the opposite effect. When Lin Biao and the Gang of Four carried out their internal struggle and internal massacre within the proletariat and people — under the guise of "class struggle" — one of the reasons for their achieving such a level of atrocity was their criticism of the "theory of human nature" and humanism. It must be pointed out that, apart from a few inhuman power seekers, many of those who took part in "class struggle," even those who actually degraded and hurt people, were basically good people. What is so sad is that these comrades actually believed they were involved in "revolutionary activity"; whoever was most cruel and thorough was most "revolutionary"! Good people punishing good people, people injuring their own, this is what "class struggle" meant during those years.

If these comrades had known that the proletariat has the task of liberating all mankind and is therefore the most conscientious humanist of all, then they would have understood why Comrade Mao Zedong repeatedly taught us not to allow physical abuse, even of the enemy. When someone invents dozens, even hundreds, of tortures to stretch a man (even if he is a real enemy — and how few they are!) on his painful journey from birth to death, then they would oppose, prevent, or at least be unwilling to join in such crimes.

There is no love or hate on Earth without reason or cause; hate is based on love, and the deeper one's love for mankind and the peo-

ple, the more burning one's hate for their enemies. For many
years, the word "love" seemed to have disappeared from our vocab-
ulary. We were incessantly told to love abstracts, but love for our
comrades, friends, wives, and husbands gradually disappeared from
our literature. This is just what Lin Biao, the Gang of Four, and
power-hungry bloodsuckers like them wanted. An atmosphere of
suspicion and hatred between people was the morality they sought!
An atmosphere of verbal abuse and of the cries of people suffering
was sweet music to their ears! Hatred became the main substance
of life, the main factor in social relations, the aim of life!

The Gang of Four made "class struggle" and "dictatorship of the
proletariat" ends in themselves. The real aim, man, became a
means, itself of no importance, something dispensable, a sacrificial
object to be placed on the altar of "class struggle" whenever con-
venient. How many loyal servants of the revolution, innocent laborers and pure young people, thus died at the hands of their comrades
and friends!

IV

The idea of the individual and individuality is also a product of
recent history and is of central interest to modern literature. An
important factor in promoting man's independence, achieving a rea-
sonably full development of his hidden potential, and maintaining a
reasonable pace of historical development is for him to enter the
stage of history with independence, dignity, and freedom.

What decides a man's value? The decision rests with the man
himself! The question was raised by progressive bourgeois thinkers
long ago. In the literary Renaissance the great poet Dante said:
"The holy seed falls not on a family, but on a single person.... It
is not his family that makes a man noble, but a man who makes his
family noble." In the seventeenth century, Montesquieu advanced
the argument:

We praise a horse not for its saddle and reins, but for its strength and speed;
a hunting dog not for its collar and kennel, but for its agility; an eagle not for
the tether and bell on its claw but for its wings. Why do we not likewise evaluate man according to his basic nature? A great retinue of retainers, a magnificent palace, enormous power and a huge income, they are all external to
him; they are not part of the man himself. You would not buy a cat in a bag;
if you buy a horse, you take off his reins for you want to see his form bare

and uncovered. Why then when you evaluate a man do you cover him up? He only shows us those parts which are not his alone, concealing that which would enable us to form a correct estimation of him. What you want to know is the worth of a sword, not its sheath...just as in ancient times someone wittily remarked: "Do you know why you think he's so tall? You've counted in his wooden shoes."

Inasmuch as they are an expression of feudal autocracy, such superficial attitudes are already historical relics in many countries (although capitalist society has certainly not allowed the complete realization of the ideals of these progressive thinkers, since for it wealth is an important measure of a man's worth). Nonetheless, here in China, both in life and in literary works, a man's worth is frequently decided by his birth, social status, service record, and job, rather than by his true integrity and ability. Before "Spring Blossoms" hardly an author touched on this problem.

To develop a man's true worth, we should give each person the conditions to unfold and develop his individuality to the full. Under the ultra-left line, however, there was an invisible force pressing conformity on people in their social life. This is just what I meant by "spiritual egalitarianism." If we ask everyone to conform to convention, know his place, never say anything surprising, and never mention anything exceptional, then the patterns of men's behavior and thought become repeats of known specimens; in the end even the language is monotonous, and all opinions (of course most come from officials) can only be expressed in some interchangeable formula. In time people not only learn and become used to hiding their true thoughts and feelings deep inside — especially those unique to themselves — but in due course they lose even the desire to make their own observations and have their own thoughts and experiences, and they no longer want to communicate their true feelings. If life is like this, how could literature not be affected? We can ask why there are so few outstanding characters in the stories and plays of those years. But when in life people have to suppress their own personalities, when strong personalities lead inevitably to strong discouragement, how can we blame literature and art? Perhaps it is only men like Chi Qun, Weng Senhe, and Zhang Tiesheng and their bosses who have truly extended and exhibited their individuality.

Now we recognize that all are equal before the law and equal before the truth. Equality was not so intolerable just because it was a product of the capitalist age; the problem was to get rid of the hypocrisy on the part of the bourgeoisie in boasting of "equality" while maintaining the system of private ownership and exploitation, and so to give "equality" its true meaning.

We have destroyed the system of man exploiting man; we now have the right to discuss human dignity, human rights, and the equality of all men in a socialist society. This is not out of some theoretical interest, but because the manifestations of feudal attitudes toward these problems have become an obstacle to the socialist modernization of our present society. Why were there so many instances of brutal commands and revenge attacks? How did "one man's word is law" and patriarchy survive? It was because certain people in positions of leadership did not consider their subordinates and the masses to be their equals, independent men with equal dignity and rights. The latter, either because they lacked awareness or for some other reasons, inevitably did not have the strength to protect themselves. This was frequently the state of affairs in the Party. The relationship between the Party secretary of a branch or committee and its members sometimes became one between superior and inferior. Anyone who disagreed with his boss was "disrespectful" or "disobedient" toward the leadership. One even saw some leading cadres freely cursing the leading cadres under them. To people like this, there was no such thing as "human dignity" or the integrity of the individual. It is hard to imagine how a man can be deprived of the respect due him and even be the object of revenge and still be happy, still devote all his ability and potential to the building of socialism!

Men curse men and men are cursed; men attack men and men are attacked — perhaps the victims often do not even think they should be protected or do not dare to protect their own rights. In pointing this out, I clearly am not advocating any abstract theory of human nature. Marxism holds that man "in reality, in his activity, is bound by the certain limits of his productivity and the level of association appropriate to the stage of its development"; man "is not in some sort of ideal place cut off from the world, living in isolation; he exists in a reality that has certain limitations, is always in the process of development, which he can observe through experience." Human nature is thus a concrete historical phenomenon. Recognizing that men have characteristics held in common, characteristics that differentiate them from animals, does not prevent us from observing man in specific historical conditions.

Lenin said long ago that, after the capitalist countries of Western Europe had their socialist revolutions, there would still be a problem for democracy requiring "extra work." In China, with its several thousand years of feudal history, where productivity, cultural level, and democratic tradition are underdeveloped, this "extra work" obviously involves much greater effort. Literature and art have a huge potential in this historical task. To destroy the various obstacles in the path of real life and in people's traditional attitudes, to enable the Chinese people to have their due dignity and rights in the various spheres of life, to stand up like masters, to take up the task of the Four Modernizations like heroes, taking the initiative with happiness in their hearts — this is the task of contemporary literature, and it will be the most vital topic in the literature of our era.

Translated by John Beyer
(Wenxue pinglun, 1979, No. 6)

12

A PERSONAL STATEMENT

Xiao Jun

In the past, I have been the subject of many diverse rumors, and they require an explanation. Explain what? you ask. Explain my goals in life, my faith in humanity, what man seeks in his ideas, and what contributes toward the attitudes people adopt.

I have four goals in life. First, I would strive to see that our great Chinese nation achieves total self-reliance; second, I would strive to see that the great Chinese people achieve total liberation; third, I would strive to see that all people everywhere in this great land — particularly the laboring classes — achieve total emancipation; finally, it is my fervent hope that the future will never again witness the appearance of a society in which exploitation or oppression of one's fellow man exists. It is of no concern to me whether these four goals, which I have held all my life, are realized in the name of socialism or of communism. These four goals have been at the heart of every word I have spoken, every job I have undertaken, every work I have written. That has been true in the past, it is true today, and it will surely be true in the days to come.

Now let me deal with my faith in humanity. I am a great believer in history. History is inexorable, reality is solemn. I am, to continue, a believer in the people, for they are sharp-sighted. Beyond that, I believe that Truth is no man's private domain and can never be wrested from the masses by brute force. Let me illustrate with a story: in the Middle Ages, the Inquisition threatened to burn Galileo at the stake; but his captors said that he could be spared if he would publicly acknowledge that the Earth did not revolve around the sun. Galileo responded by saying that the Earth did revolve around the sun and that a public denial by him would do nothing to alter the fact; this, I feel, is Truth.

I have my hopes. As a worker in the contemporary literary arena, I hope to use what strengths and abilities I possess to elevate the peoples' revolutionary values, to make them external values rather than degenerate values or values belonging to the lower orders. Someone [Stalin] once said that a writer is the engineer of the soul. How is one to go about fortifying the people's souls? Before undertaking the task of fortifying the people's souls, one must first examine one's own soul to see if it is transparent, if it is hard and unyielding — like a diamond. If our own souls fall short of the mark, I'm afraid that...

What is the soul, after all? My understanding of it has no relationship to the religious view. It is, to my way of thinking, a crystallization formed by the union during the course of a man's life of his ideals, his material possessions, his intelligence, his emotions, and his volition.

The third hope involves the arming of the people's minds. And what shall they be armed with? With the Thought of Mao Zedong. The minds of all the people must be armed with this embodiment of productive force. My fourth hope is that the collective development of our people can be accelerated. In sum, I offer up these four points in the service of our great national struggle toward revolutionary modernization.

I would also like to speak briefly about my attitude toward life. The story goes that the word "difficult" did not appear in Napoleon's dictionary. I have a dictionary of my own, one in which the word "fear" does not exist. The concept of "fear" is foreign to me. I fear other human beings least of all — what is there to be afraid of: a couple of legs? a belly? a nose? a pair of eyes? If I believe that I am right in something, even though I stand in opposition to the entire world, I'll not give in. That, in essence, is my attitude toward life.

There is, moreover, a guiding principle in my life, which I can describe as living as unobtrusively and for as long as I can. I believe that there are no barriers in the world that can stop the inevitable. Human existence can be reduced to two words — "life" and "death." If death doesn't faze you, what other barriers remain? I believe, in fact, in one simple premise: weakness is the source of all evil. Think it over.

I am a man of the thirties; I can scarcely believe that I have been consigned to thirty years of obscurity so complete that I have been ignorant of everything that has occurred around me. I have known nothing of literary or artistic accomplishments, nothing of the state of affairs in literary and artistic circles. Many prominent literary works have completely escaped my notice. My "interment" began in 1949 and I have only recently managed to claw my way back out

of the ground. My old friends from the Northeast call me an "excavated relic"; I am a walking, talking "excavated relic."

It has been difficult for me to prepare a talk for today, since I am
so out of touch. As I see it, there are outstanding debts that have
accumulated over the past thirty years, in political as well as artistic spheres. In these thirty years we have witnessed both the spring
and the winter of literary and artistic activities. But for me, in my
special circumstances, it has been a long, long winter; I have undergone a thirty-year hibernation.

What I want to talk about now is my personal winter in the heart
of spring. I am not interested in settling old scores. To whom
would I seek redress? Gao Gang? Lin Biao? They're both dead.
Scores need not be settled, but that is not to deny their existence.
As we have seen from Comrade Zhou Yang's report, over the past
thirty years we have experienced a long springtime, interrupted
only by the ten years of winter under the Gang of Four's reign of
terror. But not for me.

In 1958, long before the Gang of Four appeared on the scene, I
was subjected to a "critical reexamination," all because of a short
essay I wrote in Yan'an in the early 1940s entitled "'Love' and
'Patience' among the Comrades." The essay is still around, though
a different value has probably been placed upon it these days in light
of the constantly changing "market values" of history.

Following the critical attack on me in the Northeast in 1949, I
traveled from the Fushun Mines in Liaoning to Peking where I
wrote a novel entitled Coal Mines in May. At the time I must admit
that I probably belonged to the eulogistic faction. I sent my manu-
script to a publishing house and then sat back to await their response. After six months or so, they very politely informed me
that they had decided against publishing it. I followed that up with
the submission of an 850,000-word novel, The Past Generation. The
editorial committee wanted me to shorten it by 200,000 words, to
which I responded, "You cut 200,000 words!" That ended that. My
third submission was a historical novel entitled King Wu Vanquishes
Jiu; the fourth was another historical work entitled The Annals of
Wu and Yue. Neither gained their approval. My next step was to
tie all four manuscripts up into a bundle and send them, along with
a letter, to Chairman Mao and Premier Zhou, using my wife as a
messenger. Six months later, I received a letter from the Central
Committee of Culture and Education informing me that they had received a directive from Chairman Mao granting them permission to
"publish Xiao Jun's works." I showed the letter to Feng Xuefeng,

whose response was, "This letter is all you need — go ahead and publish them." So I authorized publication of two of the four [Coal Mines in May and The Past Generation], in both cases using my original manuscripts, the ones that had originally been rejected. Unpublishable works were thus made publishable by a single sentence from Chairman Mao. What kind of "doctrine" is this? Is it a "doctrine of publish by merit" or a "doctrine of publish by fiat?" I addressed this issue in my afterword to Coal Mines in May, the last line of which reads, "Bureaucratism is a major hindrance to production, and we must draw a lesson written in blood." I copied this word for word from an actual report in a newspaper, so as to protect myself from criticism. The publisher wanted me to change this part, but I left it exactly as it was.* As for The Past Generation, I had it published in its entirety, omitting nothing. Initially, I would have been content to have only one of my manuscripts published, but after our "litigation," I wound up with two.†

When the People's Literature Publishing House decided to reprint my Village in August [1935], they insisted that I delete Lu Xun's Foreword, saying that the styles were incompatible and that they would publish the novel only if the Foreword were deleted. I decided that in order to keep the hand it was painfully necessary to sacrifice one small finger (please don't misconstrue my metaphor as a disparagement of Lu Xun's Foreword). I didn't want anyone to think that this novel of mine would sell only if it were preceded by Lu Xun's Foreword.

It did not take long for criticism of my Coal Mines in May to appear; it was soon labeled a "poisonous weed." All future plans for printing were scrapped, and I was forced to lay down my pen and try to find a job in health services to support my family and myself. At the time, I thought back to the soldiering days of my youth and regretted ever having become a writer. I took an examination at the public health bureau for assignment as a practitioner of Chinese medicine, but nothing ever came of it. One day, out of the blue, I was directed to report for work at the Ministry of Culture, where I was assigned to the editorial committee for drama. I had previously been engaged in some archaeological work, identifying ancient artifacts and helping with tomb excavations, thereby encroaching on the realm of gods and demons.... I had also taught martial arts and

---

*This line does not appear in the 1954 Writers' Publishing House version. — Tr.

†The Annals of Wu and Yue has recently been published (1980) by the Heilongjiang People's Publishing House. — Tr.

had done other odd jobs to keep body and soul together. Eventually I was assigned to the Institute for the Study of Dramatic Arts. This distasteful experience of being shunted from pillar to post was proof positive that, for me at least, these seventeen years of literary activities belonged not to spring but to winter.

Lenin once said that without clarity of thought there can be no clarity of expression. The report delivered by Comrade Zhou Yang was of considerable length, but he skirted the issues and has left us with no clear impression of a central idea. This is particularly true in his comments on lessons to be learned beyond those pertaining to the Gang of Four. Here his report is marked by generalities presented in a coy, bashful manner, concealing rather than exposing key points and evading the issues before us. It reminded me of the little couplet, "It seems perhaps it could possibly, but I just can't say today." What it amounted to was a person unwilling to speak his mind. If this report were the work of Comrade Zhou alone, I would have a fistful of comments and recommendations, but since he is here representing a Party organization, I'll keep my mouth shut.

With the smashing of the Gang of Four, the entire literary world can bathe in the warmth of spring, and for me it is certainly the beginning of spring. Recently, the Peking Municipal Party Committee implemented a policy in my case, officially exonerating me of any past "crimes," thereby formalizing my "liberation." During my recent return trip to the Northeast, I visited twenty or more cities and gave in excess of twenty public addresses to a combined audience of more than ten thousand. I was received enthusiastically by friends, new and old, by representatives of the Party, and by local administrators. Some of them jokingly referred to me as an "excavated relic," almost as if they were celebrating the return of a "conquering hero." Not long ago I remarked to a Japanese friend that a writer who truly satisfies the needs of the people can never be vanquished, is not susceptible to intimidation, is impervious to insults and slander, is irrepressible, and cannot be submerged. But if the people do not need him, he is lost. In conclusion, I want to reiterate that I am not interested in settling old scores. However, when the time comes for me to write my memoirs, rest assured that these debts will not be overlooked.

Translated by Howard Goldblatt
(Ta-Kung-Pao — American
Edition — 11/23/79)

13

TELLING MOTHER
WHAT'S ON MY MIND

Liu Xinwu

I am very excited about being here to speak today. I am one of
the many new writers who have caught the people's attention during
the past three years. There is a great deal that I would like to say
to the leaders and elders of literary and art circles and to the comrades present here, so much that I really don't know where to begin.
This is a rare opportunity. Since time is limited, today I will address only two issues. I hope that my speech will be able to communicate the aspirations of my generation of writers, but since
there was not time to consult with the others beforehand, I take sole
responsibility for my words.

The first issue I would like to address is that of opposing "the
Left" and guarding against "the Left." As we meet at this time,
there are three perceptions that agitate us younger writers and that
are always on our minds. In the first place, prior to listening to
Comrade Zhou Yang's report the other day, we mourned those sacrificial victims who were killed by Lin Biao and the Gang of Four.
We were shocked by the sheer numbers. Some of them were sacrificed in the prime of life, while others, although older, were still
in good health when they were killed; many died very tragically.
Years ago, when the five martyrs from the League of Left-Wing
Writers were killed, it was said that they were Communists,
plotters of revolution. In other words, they were killed for being
leftists. Although they were cruelly sacrificed, I do not think that
their souls were agonized in the least. Now what sort of charges
were leveled against the sacrificial victims whom we now mourn?
"Counterrevolutionary Revisionists," "Bourgeois Reactionary Authorities," "Old Rightists," "Big Rightists," "Rightists Who Slipped
through the Net," "Sinister Gang,".... In short, they were all
turned into rightist forces and then killed. The souls of these martyrs from the fields of literature and art who never lived to see the

Gang of Four smashed certainly suffered all the agonizing torment imaginable! As we listened to their names being read and lowered our heads in silent mourning, we could not help asking questions like: Why, in a socialist nation led by the Communist Party, does committing oneself to serving the people by promoting a rich, strong literary and artistic enterprise require making mental preparations to lay down one's life? No wonder so many of my friends and relatives said to me with the best of intentions after the meeting: "Don't consider yourself fortunate to be mounting the podium. The world of literature and art is a mine field. Look at how many people were killed in the Cultural Revolution alone! Now you have stepped into that circle. Are you prepared to be blown up?"

As for the second perception, many of the writers whom we highly respected and admired in the past have suffered strokes or must now use a cane for support; some have lost the ability to speak or have become prematurely gray as a result of terrible abuse. In particular, when we see Comrade Xia Yan, who has written many fine works for the people and performed many fine deeds, but whose bones were broken by hooligans and carelessly set in the hospital, leaving him with a deformed leg, a complex emotion surges within our breasts: Why? Why did these tragedies occur? Why were so many revolutionaries and good people characterized as the most heinous of rightists — "Revisionist Elements" — then abused so cruelly?

The third perception regards the many middle-aged writers who have undergone so many hardships yet have maintained their colorful luster, whose thinking is so keen, who are so loyal and devoted to the work of the Party, the people, and the country, and who are artistically so talented and prolific. In the last three years their new works have ignited popular feeling. But just look at them: not one, or two, or even a few, but a large number were characterized as "rightists" in 1957. They were deprived of the right to write when their talents were in full bloom. This stretched on for twenty years. How many twenty-year periods do people have in their lives? They themselves said: "Being down and out for these twenty years also had its advantages, for we penetrated to the lowest levels of the people and strengthened our connection with them." Admittedly, these words are not without truth, but we novices who have just advanced into the world of literature and art cannot help pondering: Is it possible that we also must make this kind of mental preparation, to plunge into the thick of life for twenty years wearing a "rightist" cap before returning to take up our pens once more? No! This kind of thing cannot be allowed to happen again!

Experience has shown that, of the many writers who were made into rightist forces and knocked down, virtually none were true rightists. Now, as for "leftist" opportunist elements, how many were knocked down, expelled from the Writers Association, capped, and handed over for remolding under the surveillance of the masses or sent to do labor reform that resulted in injury or death? Not a single one, strangely enough. Looking at this situation and reflecting on it, we cannot help but arrive at this conclusion: We must never again blindly "oppose the Right, oppose the Right, repeatedly oppose the Right." In order to keep these tragedies from being reenacted we must oppose the ultra-left and guard against the ultraleft. In the past, ultra-leftism brought severe injury to the world of literature and art. It still poses a real threat today!

During these days of discussion, many comrades have raised the issue of a sense of security. We younger writers are equally sensitive to this issue. In the Congratulatory Message given by Comrade Deng Xiaoping, representing the Central Committee of the Chinese Communist Party, and in Comrade Zhou Yang's report, some of our works from the past three years have finally received formal approval. We know only too well that this fair and warmhearted assessment was not easily come by. After my work "The Class Counsellor" was published, there were people who said: "Don't be blinded by the sensation it has created. What about Wang Meng's 'A Newcomer to the Organization Department'? Didn't it also create a stir years ago? This is exposé literature, thaw literature!" To be sure, any sort of criticism of "The Class Counsellor" is most welcome, including this; so long as it is written in an essay with a clearly stated point of view, well-developed analysis, and articulated reasoning, it is criticism in the spirit of "a hundred schools contending." But the people who say this type of thing do not write essays; they want only to attack people and ferret out rightists. What I am telling you is not conjecture, but is based upon logical reasoning. The facts are on my side. There are still those who exert an ultra-leftist influence in literary and art circles. They not only threaten the safety of old and middle-aged writers, but the safety of us young writers as well. In the face of this kind of threat, we cannot be forbearing and conciliatory. We must rise to resist!

Honestly speaking, when confronted by the threat of ultra-leftist influence, in addition to arguing strongly on just grounds, we tender seedlings in literature also need people to step boldly forward to protect us. After our works were published, they produced strong reactions: thousands of people wrote letters to us, the great majority of which were supportive. This is a powerful backup force against ultra-leftist influence. But frankly speaking, although the principle that "the masses are the most authoritative critics of works of literature and art" has been raised, it has not been so easy to put it into practice. At the present stage of history, whether or not leading comrades of literary and art circles, critics with influence, and the old guard promptly stand up to give support still largely decides the fate of new talents and new works. I am grateful that a large number of gardeners and equerries have boldly come forward, occasionally taking great risks to give us new seedlings and thousand-li steeds their warm support and rigorous, patient guidance. Here I can represent young writers like Lu Xinhua, Kong Jiesheng, Zhang Jie, Jia Ping'ao, and Jiang Zilong in expressing heartfelt thanks to periodicals like Wenyi bao [Literary Gazette] Wenxue pinglun [Literary Criticism], Renmin wenxue [People's Literature], Renmin ribao [People's Daily], Guangming ribao [Guangming Daily], Gongren ribao [Workers' Daily], Zhongguo qingnian zazhi [China Youth Magazine], and Zhongguo qingnian bao [China Youth], because they felt duty-bound to promptly stand up and organize symposia and discussions, publish essays, and give us valuable support and guidance.

I would also like to mention two leading comrades of literary and art circles, Comrades Feng Mu and Chen Huangmei. They have done a tremendous amount of concrete work in the area of nurturing new writers. Not content to simply offer enthusiastic approval of strong points, distinguishing features, and general trends, they have also given pertinent advice regarding our weak points, shortcomings, and other unhealthy factors. Since we young writers never made the acquaintance of these two comrades in the past and have not had much individual contact with them here, our thanks to them are not swayed by any personal considerations. We hope that the Propaganda Department of the Central Committee and the Chinese Writers Association will openly commend and popularize this spirit of nurturing new talent and new works. There is merit in cultivating new flowers; it is criminal to trample on new seedlings! We await even more diligent gardeners to come forward to water, prune, and spray us, to urge us to blossom and bear fruit.

Of course, owing to our inherent faults and the varying degrees of

poison we were subjected to during the period of havoc caused by
Lin Biao and the Gang of Four, and owing to the limited nature of
our level of thought and artistic ability, our creative works are still
in a state of relative immaturity. They might even have obvious
defects. But we are willing to proceed along the road of revolutionary realism. We want to speak the truth, not lies. We offer up our
fervently innocent hearts to the Party, to our socialist motherland,
and to its beloved people. Because of this we deserve to receive
nurturing and assistance, guidance, and correction. Beloved Party,
right now there are people calling upon you to organize a new anti-
rightist movement. They want you once again to make the world of
literature and art your object of attack, to grab the "lead sheep"
and mop up the "revisionist elements," which include us tender
seedlings. Do not be taken in under any circumstances! Bear in
mind Comrade Yang Hansheng's long list of sacrificial victims who
met with tragedy and injustice. Take a look at the white hair and
wrinkles on the faces of Ba Jin, Ding Ling, and others of the older
generation and at the paralysis of Comrade Xia Yan. Look at the
eyes of Liu Binyan, Wang Meng, and the great crowd of "May Seventh" fighters who were compelled to lay down their pens for twenty years, yet have been unwavering in their attitude toward you from
the beginning. Read the millions of letters, brimming with heartfelt words, written to us young writers by our readers. You must
be vigilant! You must be careful! Your great cultural army cannot
withstand another calamity. The straightforward, sincere souls
that are faithful to you cannot be twisted and tormented anymore!
Regardless of how many times people call upon you, you must adhere to the guiding principle of "let a hundred flowers bloom and
a hundred schools of thought contend." You must oppose the "Left"
and guard against the "Left." You must not allow tragedies to be
reenacted!

As for the second issue, I would like to say something about the
view of creative work held by quite a few of us young writers, which
is that literature must struggle to eliminate the dark side of life.

In evaluating the new talents and works of the past three years,
Comrade Zhou Yang pointed out in his report that these works not
only smashed the heavy shackles placed on literary and art workers
by the Gang of Four and broke through every forbidden area that
had been set up, but also broke through the numerous prohibitions
of the seventeen years following the founding of the nation. I consider one of the most remarkable breakthroughs to be the exposure

and dissection of the dark side of life frankly, sincerely, and with an irreconcilable hatred of evil. At the outset, our works merely authentically reproduced the hand-to-hand combat between the forces of light and dark during the Lin Biao, Gang-of-Four period. There were people who could not abide this. They came out in opposition, saying that these works vilified the Great Proletarian Cultural Revolution. Then in a speech celebrating the thirtieth anniversary of the founding of the nation, Vice-Chairman Ye Jianying made a basic appraisal of the ten years of the Cultural Revolution and pointed out the extensive counterrevolutionary damage inflicted by Lin Biao and the Gang of Four, which caused such great suffering. During that period, the people were hurled into the midst of a bloody terror. This sort of entanglement is probably no longer possible in light of the appraisal that has now been made public.

Later, our works began to touch upon the lingering illnesses caused by the Gang of Four, of both the external and the internal varieties. Therefore, some people said this was "exposé literature," "literature of the wounded." Later still, works appeared that sought out the source; they began to probe into the origin and development of the ultra-leftist line taken by Lin Biao and the Gang of Four. Most recently, works about the dark side have appeared that reveal new internal contradictions among the people, touching upon bureaucracy, problems of special privileges and the legal system, the baneful influence of feudal consciousness, etc. Therefore, some people feel that our overall condition is unhealthy, as though the literary and art world were once again courting disaster, making a purge inevitable.

I consider this course of development in literary and artistic creation following the smashing of the Gang of Four to be a very natural thing. On the one hand, our Central Committee has reinstated the fine tradition of seeking truth from facts and has established the theoretical front of "practice is the sole criterion for determining truth." This will certainly spur literary and artistic creation to return, step by step, to the road of realism and to move rapidly forward along it. Realism must authentically reflect the true features of life in our society. Over the past decade, the true features of society have been this: Light has existed all along, but has been vying with darkness. For a time, the power of darkness gained the upper hand. Even now, after light has basically triumphed over darkness, there is still a considerable amount of the dark side remaining for us to struggle against and dispel. The cause is that, after experiencing a decade of soul-stirring calamity, our people are all reflecting deeply. Inasmuch as writers' reflections are frequently deeper and more rapid than ordinary people's, their works can offer deeper perceptions more quickly.

History has taught us that every time literary and artistic works appear which have the courage to intervene in life, to expose and analyze the dark side of life, and to challenge "leftist" opportunism, certain critics who specialize in wielding sticks or opportunists who write accusatory letters are likely to emerge. They employ the trick of reviling people as rightists to prove their own "leftism." They toady by holding back unpleasant information as a scheme to gain the favor and trust of leading comrades. They cry that enemy activities present a serious threat and they clamor for the launching of an anti-rightist struggle. They scheme to confuse leading comrades' basic estimation of the political situation so that in the midst of this so-called anti-rightist struggle they can scramble for a "high mark." Comrade Ke Yan accurately sketched their countenances in her speech the day before yesterday. They mark up the price and wait for the highest bidder. Even though they write anonymous letters, they never forget to include an address where they can be reached. Their intentions are crystal clear. As soon as an anti-rightist struggle has been stirred up they will reveal their true colors and, "taking a seat according to the number on the ticket," will land a government job. These people are destructive to the stability and unity of our Party and country. Haven't we suffered enough from these people? We cannot suffer this again! To be sure, there is still a difference between the great majority of them and enemies like Lin Biao and the Gang of Four. Our opposition to them, exposing the dark side of their souls, is meant to cure their illness and save them.

Some time ago, several young people spoke with me about the destructive effects of these people, indignantly advocating an anti-ultra-leftist movement; pick out a group of ultra-leftist elements, they urged, cap them, and hand them over for remolding under the surveillance of the masses, implicating even their families and giving them a taste of what it is like to be the target of an attack! I do not endorse the extreme opinions of these young people at all, but I would like to introduce everyone to this trend of social thought. I believe that this reflects the abhorrence of the broad masses of the ultra-leftist rubbish that has gravely injured the Party and the country for so many years. Naturally, we cannot employ ultra-leftist methods to oppose ultra-leftism. To be sure, we ought to speak of unity. But when there are those who carry sticks to beat people and those who are beaten, only when the former put down their sticks and cease attacking people will it be possible to unite. When there are informers and those who are set upon, only when the former abandon their odious intentions and pledge never again to inform on others will it be possible to unite. There ought to be conditions for stability and unity, especially within the ranks of the intellectuals. These conditions are: to definitely stop the disruption caused by the ultra-leftist line, to guarantee that no further anti-rightist struggles occur, to strictly implement the "Three Don'ts," and to carry out the basic principles of "blame not the speaker but be warned by his words," "correct mistakes if you have made any and be even more diligent if you have not," and "learn from past mistakes to avoid future ones — cure the illness and save the patient!"

Naturally, those who support the opposing view on the issue of exposing the dark side, like the above-mentioned "stick carriers," are in the minority. The overwhelming majority are well-meaning comrades. They worry that, if these kinds of works increase, they could give rise to unrest in the masses' thinking, intensify certain internal contradictions among the people, disturb the excellent prospect of stability and unity, or cause people to be pessimistic and depressed. Thus, they are not beneficial for promoting struggle by the masses to realize the Four Modernizations.

I wish to tell these well-meaning comrades what I know about the situation among some young people. I've come into contact with quite a few youngsters whose thinking has become very depressed. Why is this? It is because in the face of the dark side of life they have not been able to get an accurate interpretation. They thirst to read works that candidly face reality, extol the brightness and expose the darkness that actually do exist, and offer an acceptable interpretation. Do you think that by producing literature for these youngsters that is completely "eulogistic" you will be able to convince them to devote themselves to the Four Modernizations? On the contrary; by avoiding the dark side of life and deceiving them with a brightness that is exaggerated or even false, you will only drive them further into despondency, despair, and doubt. There are many young people of this type. If you want to employ forms of literature and art that arouse their enthusiasm for and devotion to the Four Modernizations, then you must produce works that speak

the truth! Only works like this can allow them to regain confidence
in eliminating the dark side of life and gain renewed motivation to
carry out the Four Modernizations. If you don't believe this, we
are willing to take the tens of thousands of letters we have received
from readers and compile them into a thick volume for your reference.

Here I would like to stand up and say a few words for those young
people who lost their precious youth during the turmoil of that decade and whose souls are covered with innumerable scars. Among
certain of the youngsters who run so-called popular [unofficial]
publications, perhaps there actually are those who have totally lost
faith in the Party and socialism, who have slipped into the quagmire
of opposition to the Central Committee and its correct line, and who
constitute counterrevolutionary elements who commit criminal of-
fenses. But the great majority of them can be understood, can be
won over, educated, and united. It is essential to arrest and convict
the tiny minority of counterrevolutionary elements whose crimes
are irrefutable; but, under no circumstances, should you expand the
net! Make our wide bosom a warm bed. Give comfort to those
countless youths whose souls are scarred. Let them rest and re-
cuperate! Even more, the works they print and the expressions of
political views they publish should not all be rejected out of hand.

I have come into contact with quite a few youngsters who object
strongly to my works. I have also read their works, and I believe
that their exposure of the dark side of society is acceptable, even
though I don't agree with their attitude, their point of view, or their
sentiments. I don't agree with their naturalistic technique of "exposure for exposure's sake." I frequently argue with them until I'm
red in the face, but they don't hold it against me and I haven't lost
faith in them either. They consider my intentions good. I believe
that the day will come when most of them will come to their senses.
I think that the contradictions between us and them can be completely resolved by discussion, criticism, and healthy competition. Look
to see who is capable of producing works that are correct, intelli-
gent, and moving and that are characterized by forthright exposure
along with incisive analysis. This way, not only will we be able to
win over the broad masses, but will also be able to win over most
of the readers of incorrect, unhealthy literature; we can even look
forward to educating those literary youth who truly have problems
in thought and consciousness and thus win them over. Right now
among the active literary youth, there are quite a few with excep-

tional talent who are willing to ponder matters and seek the truth. We only need to mobilize them appropriately and they will make substantial contributions to the development of our socialist literary enterprise!

As for the great majority of youngsters, they are full of positive energy and are fighting on the front lines to carry out the Four Modernizations. They are a generation of thinkers, a generation which demands that we produce works of art that are saturated with profound reflections on the times, on life, and on people and affairs. Since the dark side of life has not already caused them to be perplexed and downhearted, is it possible that writing about the dark side could accomplish this? It is precisely in order to dispel the dark side of life that they are carrying out such a tenacious fight. This fighting posture of theirs should rightfully receive full expression in our literature.

Naturally, creating works that struggle for the elimination of the dark side of life is a serious and formidable task. It is possible that there are some unsuccessful works, even works that are failures, among those that have already been published or presented. It is possible that their interpretations of the dark side of life are not entirely accurate, that they have this or that side effect. What do we do about this? Just because one or two works are unsuccessful, must all of them be banned? I believe that this is the worst of all possible approaches. Hadn't we better adopt the way of the great Yu when he controlled the waters? There actually is a dark side to life. Since a certain amount of dissatisfaction and impatience exists among the masses, leadership is called for: writers must be led to write works that struggle for the elimination of the dark side. If the works are written unsuccessfully or have side effects, then the means of contention must be used to carry out criticism and self-criticism, which will foster other, comparatively accurate and successful works without side effects. I sincerely hope that our leading comrades are able to understand that, when the dissatisfaction of the masses toward bureaucracy and the special privileges mentality surges up, [a policy of] allowing the publication of a relatively accurate story that assails bureaucracy or a relatively pertinent poem that criticizes the special privileges mentality often has the function of promptly allaying the internal contradictions among the people and dispelling the extremist sentiments among the masses, while promoting stability and unity.

I have personally encountered several people with extreme sentiments whose anger abated after reading a work of this type; having cheered up, they said, "Look! Publishing this type of work proves that the Central Committee understands these situations and wants to solve these problems!" The great masses of the common people of China are the most broad-minded and judicious in the world; people like them are seldom found in other parts of the world. You only need to adopt "letting go one's hold" as a guiding principle and let them dare to speak to remove the tendency toward extremist actions. As for the extremist elements of every hue and stripe who are invariably involved in causing disturbances, even if you don't publish a single piece of literature that exposes bureaucracy or criticizes the special privileges mentality, they will still want to create disturbances! Don't shut the mouths of the majority just because you are on guard against a minority! Let people speak their minds freely; the sky will not fall!

There are still so many things I would like to talk about. It has been our beloved Party, our beloved new China, and our beloved people who have nurtured me as a new writer. Before Mother, I say whatever is in my heart. Perhaps many of my ideas are incorrect. If I am wrong, then criticize and instruct me! I love you, Mother! Please give me your wisdom, strength, and trust!

Translated by Helena Kolenda
(Shanghai wenxue, 1979, No. 12)

14

MY HOPES

Xia Yan

Today I would like to summarize our experiences during the seventeen-year period and offer some remarks on the training of people in the theatrical profession.

I

I consider the relationship between art and politics to be the major issue in the examination of our past experience. Those of us who lived in the 1930s lacked a clear understanding of concepts such as "art serves politics" and "art is the tool of class struggle." Thus, in some sense, we have a certain obligation to participate in the present discussion of these kinds of issues because they were raised when the League of Left-Wing Writers and the League of Left-Wing Dramatists were founded and were intimately connected with the conditions of the struggle at the time.

The groundwork for the League of Left-Wing Writers was laid in 1929 and the organization was formally established in 1930. Perhaps our young comrades do not fully comprehend the situation in those years. In 1929, the capitalist world was hit by an unprecedented economic crisis. At this juncture, the movement for the world proletarian revolution was gaining momentum. The Chinese Communist Party was successively dominated by the lines of Li Lisan and Wang Ming, both of which were lines of leftist opportunism. This was also the heyday of leftist opportunism in the Soviet Union and Japan. Under these circumstances, the league raised the call for proletarian literature and art. This was the first call for proletarian literature and art in China following the May Fourth Movement, and it was most appropriate. Several literary associations, including the Sun Society, Creation Society, Literary Research Society, South China Society, and Art and Drama Society, united to

form the League of Left-Wing Writers. This union was also most
appropriate. The great influence that the league had on history cannot be denied. Yet, it had some leftist tendencies and was split by
factional differences carried over from the past. Many progressive, middle-road writers, such as Ye Shengtao, Zheng Zhenduo,
and Ba Jin, were not admitted into the organization. When I recently reviewed the manifesto of the league, I found that it was
tinged with leftist thought. Why were progressive writers, including
those who held middle-of-the-road and less enlightened positions,
excluded from the league?

At the time, the first United Front between the Nationalists and
the Communists had just fallen apart. The Reign of White Terror
was most severe. Because of this repression, the petty bourgeoisie
became rash and vengeful, and the League of Left-Wing Writers
took some exception to the views of the middle-of-the-road writers.
Furthermore, the Party leadership followed the leftist lines of Li
Lisan and Wang Ming, who did not attach importance to the United
Front. Therefore, in our present discussion, we must recognize
that issues such as the relationship between art and politics and
the Party's guidance of literature and art arose in China for profound historical and social reasons. When we assess what happened, we cannot lay the blame on one individual or one group. The
events that transpired reflected the trend of thought of that period.
Of course, we must also take into account that all of us were quite
young and lacked political awareness and experience.

In terms of policy and creative method, there is really an inseparable link between the literature and art produced during the seventeen years following Liberation and that of the 1930s, for we have
continued in a leftist direction. Following Liberation, the majority
of cadres from the League of Left-Wing Writers (including those in
the Liberated Areas and the Nationalist-controlled zones) joined
forces. Most of the people in charge had participated in activities
of the 1930s. Therefore, I feel that these issues should be studied
from a historical perspective. While we oldtimers are still alive,
we can join with you to clarify the issues of the 1930s; together we
can summarize our experiences and lessons from the past. I consider this to be a necessity.

During the seventeen-year period, I was criticized more than
once. I was first denounced shortly after Liberation during the
criticism of the film The Life of Wu Xun. Actually, when the director wanted to shoot the film, I remarked that "Wu Xun should

not be set up as an example." Of course, later I also criticized others. During the anti-rightist campaign in 1957, I too committed errors. Today, I would like to offer my deep apologies to those comrades whom I wrongly accused of being rightists. After 1959, I was again the object of criticism. Each person has experienced these events under different circumstances and in different environments. The causes for their occurrence were complicated and cannot be attributed to one individual. For example, we must all be held responsible for the expansion of the anti-rightist campaign. We cannot say that the disorder was created by one individual who wanted to attack others. A great many comrades in theatrical circles are present here today. At that time, many people from these circles came under attack. Prior to the anti-rightist campaign, the Ministry of Culture had lifted the ban on censured plays, allowing the performance of works like Widow Ma Opens Shop and Revenge for Killing One's Son. Then during the anti-rightist campaign, people were accused for performing these plays. Does this make sense? The Ministry of Culture should be held responsible, and, as one of the undersecretaries of the Party organization in the Ministry, I should be included. These matters cannot possibly be clarified during this congress. Certain questions can be taken up for further study by the Executive Council of the Drama Association. Fortunately, most people have been rehabilitated and cleared of all false charges; some of our comrades died during the Cultural Revolution, however, and cannot be here with us today. This grieves me deeply. As Comrade Hu Yaobang said prior to the congress, the best thing we can do is cast our past feelings into the Eastern Sea! We must unite and struggle for the flourishing of literature and art and must not be constrained by personal sentiments. I agree with Comrade Zhou Yang's view of the situation during the seventeen-year period. Throughout this period, we witnessed almost continual interference. Leftist interference was the most severe, but we also experienced rightist interference, such as the production of evil plays for a brief period beginning in 1957.

Recently, a publishing company wanted to publish a revised edition of my zawen [critical essays]. Upon looking over these works, I noticed that my essays written prior to Liberation still had a spark of vitality, while those written following Liberation were more controlled and cautious, reflecting my apprehension. Many older comrades share these feelings. Han Suyin once told Cao Yu, "The original manuscripts of your plays Thunderstorm

and Sunrise were quite good. You shouldn't have revised them.
After Liberation, you rewrote the scripts, creating works of poor
quality." Following Liberation, we supported the orthodox Party
position and overemphasized the subordination of literature and
art to politics. Quite a few people thus considered the works that
they had created in the past to be inappropriate. In brief, I hope
that we will never again worry over our personal concerns and
create unhappiness. Our opinions should be written down and
brought into the open. We must not keep our views to ourselves
and must refrain from acting pettily. This is the only way we can
preserve unity and stability.

Everyone has a clear understanding of the question of unity and
stability, which has been addressed by several comrades. If China
does not now attain unity and stability, it risks the danger of per-
ishing! Because of the destruction brought by the Gang of Four, our
national economy was once on the verge of collapse. During the
last few years, we have continued to face difficulties. There are
still numerous obstacles to the implementation of Party policy on
the agricultural and industrial fronts. Many problems must still
be resolved before the life of the masses can be improved. As
writers and artists, we bear a great responsibility in this regard.
I concur with the opinion of the leading cadres, who advocate that
literature and art must serve politics. This does not mean that,
by writing a novel or a play, we can produce a few more tons of
steel or a few more catties of grain. Literature and art can create
a new generation of people under socialism by elevating their moral
character, ideological outlook, political consciousness, and esthetic
sense. Literature and art serve socialism precisely in this way!
Whenever we write a play, we must consider the purpose of the
work to determine whether it will benefit or harm the nation and
whether it will aid unity and stability.

In the debate over restricted zones last year, I stated that there
should be none whatsoever in the choice of topics or creative methods in literary and artistic works. Yet, writers who belong to the
Communist Party or espouse patriotic and progressive views should
reserve a "restricted zone" in their hearts, which keeps them from
making their comrades suffer and their enemies joyous. Most people probably did not support my view at that time. Let me explain
it further. Certain experiences have truly made a deep impression
on us. If we write about them candidly, our works will be somewhat
more penetrating than those written in the past. I was imprisoned

for eight years and forced to write nearly a thousand confessions.
I need not mention the beatings and personal insults I suffered. A
foreign friend suggested that I describe these experiences. As a
Communist Party member and a patriot, I felt that I should not.
To reveal that fascism is still strong in China could frighten the
people. We must not follow in the steps of a certain writer from
the Soviet Union who specialized in writing about political prison
camps and went to Western countries to publish his works. This
course of action does not benefit the Chinese people, nor does it
strengthen our unity and stability.

II

After the overthrow of the Gang of Four, drama took the lead
among the various literary and art forms. Many successful plays
were created. Among these, In a Silent Place, The Future Beckons,
Authority and the Law, and Azalea were quite good, especially the
latter. Azalea depicted problems that arose when the Party shifted
the focus of its work to the Four Modernizations, and this play dared
to criticize conservative bureaucrats who are nothing more than
"yes-men." From an ideological and political standpoint, these
plays contained nothing objectionable. However, I found the works
to be unsatisfactory artistically, for they contained many flaws. In
all, I noted deficiencies, especially in language, character portrayal, and acting techniques. On viewing the production of In a Silent
Place, I had mixed reactions. On the one hand, I was delighted that
the play was being performed throughout China and would have a
widespread effect. On the other, I felt disappointed. If the playwright only could have portrayed the characters' personalities
somewhat more profoundly and changed the segments that were un-
realistic, the play would have been much better. I can cite many
similar examples. In a sense, one can say that these plays were
subjected to the pernicious influence of the Gang of Four. The influence of the Gang of Four on the theatrical world was indeed formidable. After I returned home in 1975, I listened to a broadcast
of a new production of Ten Thousand Rivers and One Thousand
Mountains. After five minutes of noise and continual shouting, I
could not bear to listen any more. When we speak, we modulate
the pitch of our voices. Shouldn't we talk to friends in a different
manner from the way we talk to family members? In an article
written after the downfall of the Gang of Four, I maintained that

seeing a play was like witnessing a fight, because plays were filled with nothing but squabbles and slogans. My comrades in the film and theatrical circles are quite aware of this.

We must thoroughly discuss the Stanislavsky issue. Since the Gang of Four presented a distorted picture of his activities, we must now separate fact from fiction. For example, there are two different accounts of his trip abroad to give performances following the October Revolution. The Gang of Four asserted that Stanislavsky feared the revolution and fled from Russia. However, according to another source, he went abroad to solicit funds to use toward the construction of his homeland following the revolution. Since this is a political issue, it should be clarified. Moreover, isn't there anything we can learn from the Stanislavsky method? Can't we learn from his theories, such as those concerning the "superobjective" and "inner behavior"? In the majority of plays performed today, we do not act out our inner feelings; we merely express them verbally. In real life, it isn't this way. A man cannot reveal all his feelings to his wife and children, keeping no secrets in his heart. Is it possible that parents tell their children about their early romance? I don't believe so. Yet, in contemporary theater, this has become routine. We are also responsible for this situation.

I have written only one play since Liberation. This was the worst piece I ever created because I worried over each sentence, wondering whether or not it would conflict with Party policy. Many playwrights assembled here have much more experience than I. To my mind, the most important guideline for a play is that it should always conform with reality and be credible to the audience. We should make the spectators feel as though the words being spoken come from their own hearts and reflect feelings they cannot express. I have read numerous foreign plays and seen many performed. In truth, I was influenced by the literature of the eighteenth century, although not profoundly enough. Had I been more deeply affected, my works would have been somewhat better.

In the current productions of spoken drama, actors and actresses only speak their lines. They do not employ facial expressions and gestures. They neither hint with their bodies not project their inner thoughts. I hope that we will pay more attention to this problem in the future.

In the early period following Liberation, we invited specialists from the Soviet Union to set up a training class for directors. Employing Stanislavsky's theories, they trained several actors and

directors in just a few years. Later, Stanislavsky was criticized
and his valuable teachings were mistakenly rejected. The role of
the director is extremely important. An inexperienced director
can create a bad production out of a perfectly good play. Converse-
ly, an experienced director can transform a mediocre play into
an excellent production. All of you here today know this principle
quite well. At present, there is a temporary shortage of actors
and directors. Yet, it is easier to find actors than directors. As
long as there are good directors, actors can receive more practical experience and better guidance and hence can be trained in a
shorter period of time. Actors from the 1930s, such as Yuan
Muzhi, Zhao Dan, and Jin Shan, did not receive their training in
professional acting schools but learned how to perform with amateur troupes. Later, under the guidance of their directors, they
improved their skills considerably and became accomplished actors. Hu Die and Ruan Lingyu informed me that they learned how
to perform in the same manner. The training of directors is much
more difficult. A director must possess considerable knowledge,
worldly wisdom, and a deep understanding of society. He must be
informed about affairs not only in China, but in foreign countries
as well. If he is completely ignorant of life in other countries, he
will be ineffective. We cannot be isolationist. While we could still
close our eyes to the rest of the world in the seventeenth and
eighteenth centuries, how can we possibly do so in the 1970s? I
hope that the circles of modern and traditional drama will pay close
attention to the training of directors.

I also advocate the study of classical Chinese literature. In middle school, I memorized dozens of selections from the Guwen
guanzhi and several Tang poems. However, when I was nineteen,
I joined the May Fourth Movement. At that time, the great trend
toward Westernization was under way, so I set aside my classical
texts and began to study Western European literature. All the famous actors I knew, including Mei Lanfang, Chen Yanqiu, and Xun
Huisheng, read many foreign works. Zhou Xinfang was well known
for being an avid reader. His entire house was piled with books.
He read all kinds of literature.

I did not devote myself to the serious study of classical Chinese
writings until after Liberation. Compelled by my duties in the
Ministry of Culture, I felt that reading was an absolute necessity
and made an effort to read for one or two hours every day after
work. Of course, I was not in the same league as my comrades

Guo Moruo and Mao Dun. When Mao Dun took his position as a low-ranking editor at Commercial Press at the age of nineteen, he had already read the pre-Qin philosophers, could compose highly ornate rhyme prose, and could translate from English into Chinese. I feel that young people in their twenties and thirties nowadays are much more politically and ideologically astute than people of my generation were at the same age. However, in terms of scholarship and cultural background, they are somewhat less advanced. Once I asked a young actor to recite the Song of the Great Wind by Chen Baichen. He did not recognize many characters in the text. Furthermore, since it was written in classical language, he could not make any sense out of what he had read. We should think deeply about this; Chinese people should be acquainted with the literature and art of antiquity. In my youth, I read many foreign books, including works on dramatic theory like G. E. Lessing's Hamburgische Dramaturgie. After Liberation, however, I read the dramatic theories of Li Yu and Jiao Xun. I felt much closer to their writings than those from abroad and thus derived more benefit from their works. I hope our young comrades bear this in mind. The new culture has developed from the old. We cannot break the ties with our national heritage. Some film actors of the 1930s imitated what they saw in foreign films. Thus, their movements were awkward for they did not conform to Chinese behavior. In brief, we must study our tradition so that our drama will flourish even further and reach even greater heights.

Foreigners whom I have met often ask, "Why haven't any great writers like Lu Xun, Mao Dun, and Cao Yu appeared in the thirty years since Liberation?" After careful reflection, I realize that this is a valid question. People in their fifties and sixties today were in their twenties and thirties before Liberation, at a time when they should have been progressing in their studies. But years of war and chaos made that impossible. "Since the past is behind us, we had best pursue the future." From now on, we should double our efforts and make up for lost time. Marx studied Russian at the age of sixty and was later able to read Russian works. Comrade Xu Teli began to learn French when he was forty-three and was able to read French books by the time he reached fifty. "If we are idle in our youth, we will suffer the consequences when we grow old." This is my feeling at this moment. I lack knowledge today because I read too little in the past. I hope that comrades who are still young will read more, at least a couple of hours a day. It is

my understanding that today some comrades in the fields of literature and art merely run about outdoors and read no books or newspapers. People like this are dangerous. If their numbers increase,
the cause of literature and art will be harmed.

We must take into account that the production forces of the nation
are lagging behind considerably. In order to realize the Four Modernizations, we must assimilate foreign experience and move forward. We must devote great care to the training of our people to
meet the demands of the Four Modernizations. In the early stage
of national construction, we trained a group of young film directors
like Xie Jin, Guo Wei, and Xie Tieli. They have been the most influential figures in all the film studios. It's a pity that more
weren't trained! Let's suppose that one hundred directors were
trained in the early days of national construction. Even if thirty
had been lost during the Cultural Revolution, the strength of those
who survived would still have been considerable. Our generation
must be held responsible for not making sufficient efforts in that
period. Premier Zhou told me repeatedly that we needed to train
directors and actors. He often said that contemporary actors were
deficient in the basic skills. Since they could not sing, they had to
be dubbed. They could neither ride horses nor swim. They were
ignorant of other professions and specializations. Premier Zhou
instructed us to broaden the education and training of our actors.
Once, when filming an opera, the director felt that an actor's appearance was not suitable for a part and decided to replace him
with another performer. He intended to dub the voice of the replacement with that of the actor originally cast for the part. When
Premier Zhou learned of this, he criticized us angrily.

In conclusion, unless we make a greater effort to learn, rather
than continue in an undisciplined fashion, we will experience great
difficulty within a few decades. As I mentioned during the film
congress, while China lags behind the advanced nations in the field
of science by twenty to thirty years, the disparity in the cinematic
arts is not so great, for we are only ten to fifteen years behind. I
hope that in the 1980s our films will be among the most advanced
in the world. I am placing my hopes in all my comrades in the
theatrical circles. I hope that everyone will work hard to approach
or achieve the highest standards of excellence in the coming decade.

Translated by Wendy Locks
(Renmin xiju, 1979, No. 12)

15

CLOSING ADDRESS TO THE THIRD CONGRESS OF THE CHINESE WRITERS ASSOCIATION

Ba Jin

Having completed all of the items on its agenda, the Chinese Writers Association must now ring down the curtain on its Third Congress.

The congress has been in session for six and a half days, during which the Congratulatory Message by Comrade Deng Xiaoping, the report of Comrade Zhou Yang, and the speech by Comrade Mao Dun have been discussed and analyzed in plenary sessions and in committee. Our members have spoken their minds freely during the heated discussions, holding nothing back, and the enthusiasm has been amply attested to by the frequent outbursts of applause during the reports.

Following several rounds of discussion, everyone present has been brought up to date on the achievements gained and lessons learned during the past thirty years of literary and artistic endeavor. As writers and artists, we are equally clear about our future responsibilities, are filled with confidence, and are prepared to meet the future with unbridled courage. The problems we have been discussing will surely be resolved through the constant application of the creative process during the coming weeks and months.

We have elected a new leadership for the Association. From the report by the Preparatory Committee, we have learned that a great many checks have been written against future endeavors, each of which I am confident will be cashed in the coming days. My confidence stems from the fact that the Writers Association is not a yamen exercising control over writers; rather, it is our own organization, and not just in name alone.

The present state of affairs in literary and artistic circles gives me cause for optimism. In the three years following the smashing of the Gang of Four, literary journals of every size and description have begun publication in virtually every province and major city throughout the country, and high-quality writings have graced the pages of each of them. This is unprecedented in recent history. Talented new authors of fine works have appeared all across the land. Their works are distinguished by diverse themes and unique styles, with the result that contemporary life is being viewed in a panoramic and penetrating fashion, expressing an intensity of emotions.

There are, in addition, large numbers of writers whose pens had gathered dust under coercive influence for ten or even twenty years, but who have once again begun writing highly moving works. These new and reemerging writers, all of whom are trailblazers, were steeled and tempered by events of the past. In his report, Comrade Zhou Yang said: "To meet the needs of literary undertakings in a nation of our size, we need more than just several or even dozens of such trailblazers — we need hundreds and thousands of them." These intrepid trailblazers are the force that will smash all fetters that bind the spirit and will obliterate all restricted areas. There are already many such trailblazers among us, and their ranks are constantly being swelled. I see in them bright prospects. The task before us is to implement the policy of "letting a hundred flowers bloom." Based on the current rate of progress, as long as no one interferes in the creation of our literary works or launches attacks on our writers, a flourishing period of socialist literature will emerge within a very few years. I am particularly optimistic in this regard. The "springtime of literature and the arts" of which Comrade Mao Dun sang has nearly arrived.

Some may wonder: Before the springtime arrives, must we first suffer through cold winds and frost? This question brings to mind two recent incidents. I was told during an interview with an overseas Chinese writer that she had asked other people in similar interviews to relate their hardships during the ruthless reign of the four vermin. When she asked whether or not they thought that another group like the Gang of Four could appear on the scene, the unanimous response was that it was possible. I don't know what type of people she interviewed, but my reply was different. I said that it was entirely possible that it could happen, but just as possible that it could not. It all depends on whether or not we are willing to face persecution. If our systems of democracy and law are weak or imperfect, anything could happen. The real question facing us is whether or not we are willing to once again let our pens be wrenched out of our hands! Have we the courage to hold onto our pens for dear life?

The second incident involves a book I read recently entitled
Fresh Flowers Abloom Again, an anthology of literary works
labeled "poisonous weeds" in 1957. Although they were considered
good by the majority of contemporary readers, a good deal of controversy surrounded them. Before long, an [anti-rightist] campaign was mounted and the works became "poisonous weeds." Their
authors were not only deprived of their privilege to write, but were
branded as criminals as well. Some even lost their families
through separation or death. The unreasonable and unfair punishment of these writers was met with acceptance and acquiescence
by the rest of us, or, even worse, wholehearted approval. At the
time we were unwilling or afraid to distinguish between right and
wrong. Maybe we were all just playing it safe, but the conduct of
an honest writer reflects his own conscience. Eventually it was
our turn to get exactly the same treatment as those who came before us. Today, as we look to the future with incomparable faith,
our thoughts constantly return to the countless talented writers
who died so cruelly. They too raise the call: "That historical
tragedy must never be repeated!" We should therefore have no
lingering fears. What else is there to be afraid of?

We now have a Constitution that is endorsed by the entire nation.
It is the basis of fundamental law. The Constitution guarantees our
people the freedom to engage in the study of science, to create literary and artistic works, and to engage in other cultural activities.
These are not empty words. A new criminal code will go into effect
on January 1 of next year. In his Congratulatory Message, Comrade
Deng Xiaoping said: "Writers and Artists must have the freedom
to choose their subject matter and method of presentation based
upon artistic practice and exploration. No interference in this regard can be permitted." With this as a basis, as long as a literary
work does not violate a section of the criminal code and complies
with Party doctrine, the authors' rights cannot be arbitrarily taken
away by anyone. We writers must comply with the law and not interfere with anyone else's rights. At the same time, we also have
the right to protect our own rights.

I hope that the leadership of all literary departments and organizations will cherish the talented people and will respect all writers
and their labors. In this great nation of a billion people, our problem is not a surplus of writers but a scarcity, a true scarcity!

When I attended the First Congress of Chinese Writers and Artists thirty years ago, I wrote an open letter to the literary and ar-

tistic workers of the People's Liberation Army, in which I said: "The knowledge that writers and artists like you live and work in new China makes me proud to be a writer." Today at this congress I see a great new force of young and middle-aged writers — men and women of courage, conscience, talent, and responsibility, who dare to think and to write, who have great creative powers, and whose hearts overflow with fervent love for the motherland and the people — and once again I feel it is an honor to be a Chinese writer.

My life will soon come to an end and there is little time left for me to write. But a fervent hope continues to burn in my heart, and I still harbor an intense love for the motherland and for our incomparably decent people. I will never willingly lay down my pen; I yearn to unite with all of you to carry out our responsibilities and march ever forward. As writers we should always be responsible to the people and to history. I now understand more clearly than ever that a writer of integrity and conscience cannot, by any stretch of the imagination, be shortsighted, cowardly, or timid.

What I have said today represents my own personal opinions.

Finally, on behalf of all the representatives attending the congress, I would like to express our heartfelt appreciation to all of the workers and guest-house employees. Without these comrades' round-the-clock labors, our meetings could not have run as smoothly or achieved such a high degree of success.

I now declare that this congress has come to a successful close.

Translated by Howard Goldblatt
and Judi Wong
(Wenyibao, 1979, Nos. 11–12)

16

CLOSING ADDRESS TO THE FOURTH CONGRESS OF CHINESE WRITERS AND ARTISTS

Xia Yan

Through the concern of the Party and the concerted efforts of those in attendance, the Fourth Congress of Chinese Writers and Artists and the congresses of the various associations have completed their agendas; the congress has been a success, and today it is to close. During the congress there have been various differing opinions on some questions, which require discussion in greater depth in the future. The agenda has me slated to give a closing address. As of October, I became an octogenarian, and this congress may be the last that I shall be able to attend. Thus, emulating the practice of Comrade Mao Dun, I would like to take this opportunity to talk about a few of my own views.

1. ON EMANCIPATION OF THOUGHT

The question [of emancipation of thought] was well discussed in the reports of Comrades Deng Xiaoping, Hu Yaobang, Mao Dun, and Zhou Yang. What I would like to say is that, even though no one openly opposed the necessity of the emancipation of thought in literature and art in the meetings of the China Federation of Literary and Art Circles and the various associations, I nevertheless feel that there are still those who are suspicious and fearful of or even opposed to the emancipation of thought. And this is precisely because this past year's discussion in literary and artistic circles of "practice as the sole criterion for determining truth" has not been sufficiently penetrating; it is precisely because the Summary concocted by Lin Biao and Jiang Qing has not been seriously criticized. I say this because not long ago a cold wind blew through literary and artistic circles: some set the emancipation of thought and democracy in literature and art against the "Four Musts"; others even blamed excesses in the emancipation of thought for the social upheaval created by a small handful of scoundrels and anarchists. I find such views extremely harmful, first because they do not coincide with the true situation in literature and the arts, where emancipation of thought has hardly been excessive but has only just begun to rear its head and is still some distance away from achieving full realization; and second because, since China has endured more than two thousand years of feudal government, even though the May Fourth movement did oppose Confucian-Mencian doctrines of propriety and advocated the emancipation of the individual personality, it nevertheless failed to destroy the twisted and gnarled roots of the entire feudal ideological system.

Because of the continuing widespread influence of feudal ideology and culture in China as well as the long-implemented ultra-leftist line of Lin Biao and the Gang of Four and the strictures of new and old dogmatisms, practice has proven that a true emancipation of thought in Chinese literature and art is definitely not a question that can be resolved in a short time. In this regard, we oldsters who have gone through it all have indeed experienced a great deal, from the cutting off of queues in the 1911 Revolution to the writing of essays in the colloquial speech and the adding of punctuation marks after the May Fourth movement, and even these trivial matters involved fierce and protracted struggle. And today, as the emphasis in Party and government work shifts to the Four Modernizations, our thinking must undergo enormous and profound change. Marx said that " 'Spirit' is in sorry straits right off, for it is condemned to be subject to materialist 'entanglement.'" Marx, Engels, and Lenin often quoted a famous dictum of Goethe which goes, "Dear friend, the tree of life is ever green, but theory is gray." This phrase is quite well put. It explains the relationship between matter and spirit and shows that life is the fount of theory. The tree of life is ever green — and theory? Theory is subordinate to life. This is not a derogation of theory but rather a revelation of the inherent relationship between the two. I think that this phrase is applicable to the great theory of Marxism-Leninism.

It has been more than a hundred years since Marx and Engels created Marxism, whose fundamental principles — namely, dialectical materialism, historical materialism, and the inevitable superseding of the capitalist society by the socialist society — are all truths that have been or are now being proved in practice in various aspects. But Marx and Engels lived during the nineteenth century, and so the production relationships that they were able to see were those of premonopoly capitalism, primarily the steam-powered locomotive and ship and belt-driven machinery; they never saw the reality of productive force developed through the widespread large-scale utilization of electric or atomic power. Lenin saw electric generators and electrically powered systems and said, "Communism is the Soviet regime plus national electrification." Such a statement would clearly have been impossible in Marx's day, but if someone were to utter the same words today it would seem inappropriate. Were Lenin here today, he might say that communism was the Soviet regime plus the electronic computer.

That capitalism must certainly perish and socialism flourish is a fundamental credo of Marxism, but in Marx's and Engels's day the particular ways and means by which socialism was to be established were no more than untested theory. More than sixty years of practice have proved that there has never yet been an instance of the complete and successful establishment of socialism. Therefore, in cleaving to the socialist road, it is necessary to make constant adjustments in accordance with the basic tenets of Marxism-Leninism—Mao Zedong Thought and based upon contemporary realities. Such cases are quite numerous. After the October Revolution the Soviet state first implemented a military communism with regard to the peasants, and in the subsequent changeover to the implementation of new economic policies the struggles were extraordinarily bitter. By adopting labor-exchange teams, mutual assistance groups, and cooperatives, our own Party, borrowing from the Soviet experience and beginning from China's realities, was able to rapidly bring about the collectivization of agriculture without undue change in the farming villages and without lowering production. This was not a contravening of Marxism-Leninism but rather a further developing of Marxism-Leninism by our Party. If Marxist-Leninist theory is to retain its enormous guiding role, it must develop along with life's changes.

Many who have gone abroad for observation in recent years have been astounded by the rapid development of the industrial technology of the Western nations and Japan. This reminds me of a paragraph from Marx:

> When a society's material productive forces develop to a certain stage, then contradictions will arise ... in the production relationships which have been extant and active among them, whereupon these production relationships will change from developing forms of productive force to fetters on productive force.

In 1929 the capitalist system encountered the most severe economic panic in history; at that time we all felt that this "moribund" social system was actually impeding the development of its own productive forces. Yet, strangely enough, although this capitalist system has been subject to incessantly recurring economic depression from the middle of the 1960s until now, not only has it not created a major recession of productive force, but because of the continual development of new science and technology there has appeared in these imperialist nations a great growth of industrial production. This new situation of the imperialist nations has given Marxist-Leninist theory a new topic for study.

The world is changing, societies are changing, and people's thought must also change to adapt to changes in objective reality. Writers and artists must directly confront the reality of the current rapid changes in our country and examine the literary and artistic theories to which we have grown accustomed; we cannot continue to use the same old approach. During this congress we have touched upon many theoretical questions that must be studied: for instance, whether literature and art must serve politics; whether they are subordinate to politics; whether they may be summarily regarded as nothing more than tools of the class struggle; whether all ideologies are superstructures on an economic foundation; the question of the creative method of socialist literature and art (that is, the combining of revolutionary realism and revolutionary romanticism); the question of eulogizing versus exposing; and such questions as feudal prerogatives and bureaucratism in the diversification of subject matter, and so on. We need to courageously confront reality and conduct a serious, factual study of such questions.

After Liberation, we often said that China had finished her anti-imperialist, anti-feudal, New Democratic Revolution, and so for the past thirty years there has been insufficient emphasis in literature and art on the task of opposing feudalism. In the past we often regarded the "contending of a hundred schools of thought" as nothing more than a part of the struggle between the proletariat and the bourgeoisie; yet the practice of thirty years has proven that, aside from these two factions, feudalism has been stubbornly impeding social progress in China all along. Thus, in order to clear the way for the realization of the Four Modernizations, I feel that, just as we oppose bourgeois individualism, anarchism, and factionalism of every stripe and hue, so should we include opposition to all forms of feudalism — such as paternalism, special privileges, forced unanimity of opinion, nepotism, bureaucratism, and so on — among the important tasks of our literary and artistic work. Of course, works reflecting such subject matter must have clear and definite goals and be appropriately couched. Like journalism, literature has its special sensibilities, and here we are dealing with the question of stability and unity and of remaining ever mindful of the larger view; for today the goal of emancipating thought is to benefit the people and our socialist Four Modernizations.

2. ON STABILITY AND UNITY

When we speak of stability and unity, we are in fact dealing with the question of strengthening unity in literature and the arts. Even though there were shortcomings and differences of one kind or another in our revolutionary ranks of writers and artists both before and during the War of Resistance to Japan and before and after Liberation, it must be said that we were unified as far as the general overall direction was concerned. But that bunch of scoundrels, Lin Biao and the Gang of Four, were forging alliances and collusions, creating factionalism, and destroying the unity of our ranks. In the "shedding of disorder and returning to the true path" of the past three years the backlog has been cleared away and things have improved somewhat, but among our ranks there remain personal favoritism and factional sentiment; especially in need of eradication are those bad habits fostered by Lin Biao and the Gang of Four such as serious individualism, the establishing of rankings and orders of precedence, and vying for fame, status, and a good salary. We hope that after the present congress it will be possible to get rid of the personal favoritism of the seventeen-year period and the Cultural Revolution once and for all, to thoroughly wipe out all factors that hinder unity, and to concentrate our main efforts on artistic creativity and theoretical research, in order to enable our ranks to become dauntless and iron-hard in the new Long March to implement the Four Modernizations.

At the symposium for five professions convened in May of this year by the Ministry of Culture, Comrade Hu Yaobang said that Lin Biao and the Gang of Four had brought the Chinese ship of state to the brink of either foundering or running aground, and only through the destruction of the Gang of Four by the Party was this ship saved from sinking. This reminds me of two old sayings: "Those in the same boat weather the storm together" [fengyu tongzhou] and

"Those in the same boat aid one another" [tongzhou gongji]; and so here I should like to say a few words about the larger situation. We all know that by 1976 Lin Biao and the Gang of Four had already brought our people's economy to the brink of collapse. This was also true in cultural areas. Through three years of effort, not only has this scarred and battered ship bearing 900 million people managed to stay afloat, but by dint of urgent and firm measures it has already begun to move forward through wind and waves. However, because of the severity of the destruction, it will be some time yet before repairs are complete, and to seek rapid progress in such circumstances is inappropriate.

From the demise of the Gang of Four to the Third Plenum of the Eleventh Party Congress, the Party's Central Committee has managed to accomplish an enormous amount of work, resolving many long-standing injustices and mistakes and adjusting and strengthening various aspects of culture, education, and science. Every one of us "in the same boat" must bear the burden of responsibility for mutual forgiveness and assistance, for "aiding one another." Today we have enemies, both foreign and domestic, who are most interested in our internal unrest. Some Western propaganda organs repeatedly harp on our internal wrangling and temporary difficulties without taking the trouble to find out and report the details, whereas they often remain silent or fail to give factual reports when it comes to our solidarity and accomplishments. For instance, they barely touched upon such a major event as Vice-Chairman Ye Jianying's address on the occasion of the thirtieth anniversary of the People's Republic. Is this not indeed cause for concern and alarm?

In literary and artistic work and in theoretical studies there should be no restricted areas, but I believe that before setting pen to paper a patriotic writer, a progressive writer, and especially a writer who is a member of the Communist Party will certainly consider how to so render the themes, events, and characters in which he is interested as to make them contribute toward rousing the revolutionary spirit and raising moral and esthetic levels; he must be aware of the heavy burden of responsibility he bears for the motherland and the people.

3. ON QUALITY IN LITERATURE AND ART

I should like to mention that over the past three years China's literary and artistic endeavors have won initial successes, the most notable achievements occurring in the short story, drama, and poetry. I shall not instance here those works mentioned by Comrade Zhou Yang in his report. We must admit that all of these works are capable of emancipating thought, of breaking the old strictures, and many have been acclaimed by readers and audiences. Yet we must also be aware that even in the best-received works there are more than a few shortcomings in artistic technique and skill; this is of course related to the authors' ideological levels and life experiences, but it cannot be denied that the authors' cultural education is also directly involved. In this regard, we cannot blame the young and middle-aged writers. Writers now in their fifties should be at the peak of their productivity; yet at the time of Liberation they were but youths of twenty, and during the twenty years before Liberation they underwent the upheavals of ten years of civil war, eight years of the War of Resistance against Japan, and three years of Liberation struggle. Thus, with few exceptions, they never got the chance to establish a solid literary or artistic foundation. Our writers, especially the young and middle-aged ones, should continue to deeply penetrate life while intensifying and enhancing their literary and artistic education. I quite agree with what Comrade Mao Dun said on November 3:

The young and middle-aged writers of today must not only further educate themselves with regard to the aspects of carrying on and emulating [the literary tradition]; they must not only further educate themselves in the areas of Chinese history and the history of the various nations of the world; but they must also absorb the above-mentioned knowledge in international politics, economics, and modern science.

Otherwise, it will be impossible to produce writers like Lu Xun, Guo Moruo, Mao Dun, and Ba Jin in the near future. In terms of age I am but a few years Comrade Mao Dun's junior, but in terms of cultural education there is a greater distance between us. When he was in his twenties, Comrade Mao Dun had already read the works of the pre-Qin philosophers and could compose fine couplets and even translate literary masterpieces from English. As for myself, although I had read some of the classics while in secondary school, the May Fourth Movement occurred when I was nineteen, and with it there came a "complete Westernization"; thus I was soaked in the "dye vat" of nineteenth-century European and Russian literature. I have no regrets, for this soaking enabled me to acquire

a rudimentary knowledge of European and Russian literature, but
because of this I remained before Liberation almost totally ignorant
of China's literary tradition, including everything from the Classic
of Poetry through Tang poetry and Song verse to Yuan drama, as
well as such indispensable aspects of Chinese literary theory as
prosody and drama. Forced by the exigencies of my work, I began
the study of the abundant wealth of Chinese literature only after
Liberation. This is a matter of [realizing that] "if we are idle in
our youth, we will suffer the consequences when we grow old."
China has now entered a period of stability and unity, and writers
and artists need no longer cringe in fear of political movements
like that of 1957. For those middle-aged authors faced with the
question of furthering their education, and for the young authors,
this is an excellent opportunity, one that is not to be missed. I am
glad to see that quite a few of our young and middle-aged authors
not only have emancipated their thinking but also possess literary
and artistic skills and have reached a fairly high cultural level. It
is my hope that after this congress the China Federation of Literary
and Art Circles and the various associations will take prompt steps
to define programs for creating a pervasive atmosphere of love of
study and contemplation, of diligence and hard work in literary and
artistic circles, so that in ten or twenty years — that is, by the
time our motherland has achieved the Four Modernizations — our
literary and artistic circles will be able to produce a goodly number
of excellent works worthy of our motherland and of the times.

   Lastly, I have been asked by the congress to express heartfelt
gratitude to those organizations such as the Party Central Committee, the subordinate organs of the Ministry of State, the city of
Peking, and the Liberation Army, who have given us their enthusiastic assistance in order that the congress might be successfully
completed, and also to those comrades who have unflaggingly and
unstintingly labored so that the congress might proceed smoothly.

Translated by Philip Robyn
(Wenyibao, 1979, Nos. 11–12)

About
the
Authors

Ba Jin (Pa Chin), born in 1904 in Chengdu, Sichuan, is one of
China's best known and most prolific modern writers. The son of
an extremely wealthy and powerful merchant, his rebellious spirit
led him to an acceptance of anarchism. Among the dozens of novels
and short-story collections Ba Jin wrote in the 1930s and 1940s,
his best known and most influential work was the autobiographical
novel Family (1933). He is still among the most active and productive literary figures in China; following the death of Mao Dun
in 1981, Ba Jin was named the acting chairman of the Chinese
Writers Association.

Bai Hua (Pai Hua), who was born in Henan in 1930, began writing
in 1946, although it was not until 1951 that his works first gained
national attention. He is known primarily as a dramatist and movie
scriptwriter. In 1981, he was attacked in print by a People's Liberation Army (PLA) literary critic, and even though the central
government rebuked the critic for the nature of his criticism, the
"Bai Hua Incident" soon evolved into a nationwide campaign, with
Bai Hua standing as a symbol for the "dangerous" course being
taken by at least a segment of the contemporary writing community.

Chen Dengke (Ch'en Teng-k'e) was born in Jiangsu in 1919
to an impoverished family. In 1945, he became a journalist;
his literary career began in 1946. Among his best known
works are the novels Living Hell (1950), Auntie Du (1948), and
Children of the Huai River (1954). Immediately prior to the
Cultural Revolution he was particularly active in the production
of movie scripts; he recommenced work in this area in 1978
and is currently working on a major novel set in the wartime
years.

Deng Xiaoping (Teng Hsiao-p'ing) was born in Sichuan in 1904. He is China's vice-premier and vice-chairman of the Chinese Communist Party.

Ke Yan (K'e Yen), poet and assistant chief editor of the magazine Poetry, was born in 1929 in Nanhai, Guangdong (Kwangtung). A drama major, she graduated from the Suzhou College of Social Education. Sine 1949 she has worked as an actress and playwright at the China Youth Art Theater and China Children's Theater, both in Peking. Among her more important works are the poetry collections Big Red Flower, The Most Beautiful Picture Album, Stories for Young Pioneers, and Where Are You, Premier Zhou?; the plays Flying Away from Earth and Crystal Cave; and reportages In Pursuit of the Sun and Special Representative.

Liu Baiyu (Liu Pai-yü), who is known for his reportage and fiction on military life, was born in 1916 in Peking. Attracted to Yan'an in 1938, Liu actively participated in cultural propaganda work, which took him back and forth among the guerrilla strongholds in North China. His experiences with the New Fourth Army provided the raw material for some of his best writing, collected in Flames Ahead (1959) and other works. During the Cultural Revolution, Liu was sentenced to nine years of manual labor, gaining rehabilitation in 1975. In 1977, he was appointed chief of the Cultural Department, Political Bureau of the PLA. He is currently a vice-chairman of the Chinese Writers Association.

Liu Binyan (Liu Pin-yen), born in Jilin (Kirin) Province in 1925, is best known for his journalistic writing. During the Hundred Flowers period, he published two short works that were severely criticized in the 1957 anti-rightist campaign. He subsequently spent four years as a manual laborer in the countryside. Following nine years with the newspaper China Youth, Liu was sent to a May Seventh Cadre School, reemerging in 1977 after the fall of the Gang of Four. His most influential recent piece, "Between Men and Ghosts," created a storm of controversy in its exposure of corruption among the contemporary bureaucracy. He is currently assigned to the Academy of Social Sciences in Peking.

Liu Xinwu (Liu Hsin-wu), born in 1942, is a native of Chengdu, Sichuan. Although he had published nearly seventy stories and

articles prior to the Cultural Revolution, it was his 1977 story
"The Class Counsellor" that ushered in the literary genre known
as "literature of the wounded" and established Liu as the spokes-
man for a new generation of writers. This was followed by a number of similar anti-Gang of Four works, such as "A Place for
Love." In 1979, Liu became an editor for the literary periodicals
October and Juvenile Literature.

Mao Dun (Mao Tun) was born in Zhejiang Province in 1896.
After serving as a proofreader for the prestigious Commercial
Press, he was one of the founders (in 1920) of modern China's
first major literary society, the Literary Research Association.
His own literary career began in 1928 with the publication of the
trilogy Eclipse. He was one of China's most active novelists prior
to and during the War of Resistance, gaining a reputation as the
foremost practitioner of "realism." His best-known work is the
novel Midnight (1933). Mao Dun became Minister of Culture following the establishment of the PRC in 1949, a post he held until
1964. He was, at the time of his death in March 1981, vice-chairman of the All-China Federation of Literary and Art Circles and
chairman of the Chinese Writers Association.

Wang Meng was born in Peking in 1934. He first came into
prominence with the publication of his novel Long Live Youth
(1953). His short story "A Newcomer to the Organization Department," published in 1955 during the Hundred Flowers period, became one of the principal targets of criticism during the anti-
rightist campaign that ensued. In 1963, Wang went to Xinjiang,
where he studied the Uighur language and taught school for sixteen
years. Following the fall of the Gang of Four, he recommenced
his writing career and has since become one of the leading figures
in China's current literary scene. In 1980, Wang was in residence
at the Writers' Workshop at the University of Iowa.

Xia Yan (Hsia Yen) is a native of Hangzhou in Zhejiang Province.
He was born in 1900. After returning from studies in Japan in the
1920s, he helped organize a dramatic society in Shanghai and then
was the prime figure in the establishment of the League of Left-
Wing Dramatists (1930). Among his best received and most influential plays are Sai Jinhua (1936), The Life of Qiu Jin (1940), Under
Shanghai Eaves (1941), and the Fascist Bacilli (1945). He became

an important literary official in the PRC as vice-minister of culture and vice-chairman of the All-China Federation of Literary
and Art Circles. He suffered considerable mental and physical
abuse during the Cultural Revolution but has since been rehabilitated and has resumed his official posts.

Xiao Jun (Hsiao Chün), born in 1907, is a native of Liaoning.
After a brief career in the military, he began to write in Harbin
in the early 1930s. His first novel, Village in August, published
with the help of Lu Xun (Lu Hsün), established him as one of the
foremost anti-Japanese writers and the best known of the Northeastern Group of Writers. Other works include the novels The
Third Generation (1937), Coal Mines in May (1954), and several
anthologies of short stories, essays, and poetry. He currently
lives in Peking, where he is compiling volumes of reminiscences
and other historical materials. He visited the United States in 1981.

Zhou Yang (Chou Yang), born in 1908 in Hunan, is one of the
most influential cultural and propaganda officials of the PRC. In
the early 1930s, as a member of the Chinese Communist Party,
he played a leading role in the left-wing literature and art movement in Shanghai. During the War of Resistance he was dean of
the Lu Xun Academy of Arts and president of Yan'an University.
He has served as vice-director of the Propaganda Department of
the Central Committee of the Chinese Communist Party, vice-
minister of culture, vice-chairman of the All-China Federation
of Literary and Art Circles, and vice-chairman of the Chinese
Writers Association. His views on art and literature have been
regarded as the official line of the Chinese Communist Party. In
the 1950s he was responsible for the purges of several prominent
literary figures; he himself was purged at the beginning of the
Cultural Revolution in 1966 and was not rehabilitated until 1973.

About
the
Translators

John Beyer received his B.A. from Cambridge. He continued his study of Chinese at Université Paris 7, Beijing Languages Institute, and as a visiting scholar at the University of California at Berkeley. He is currently a researcher for Amnesty International and is working on a Ph.D. dissertation at Leeds University on the peasant writer Zhao Shuli.

George Cheng, who holds an M.S. degree in Library Science (Oregon) and an M.A. in Chinese (San Francisco State), is a librarian at San Francisco State University. He has written extensively in Chinese and has published several works in both Chinese and English, including his translation of Howard Goldblatt's Hsiao Hung.

Stephen Horowitz, who received his M.A. in East Asian Studies from Stanford University, works at the Chinese Culture Foundation in San Francisco, where he is engaged in research on Chinese films.

Helena Kolenda received her A.B. in Chinese Language and Literature from the University of California at Berkeley. She is currently teaching English in Hangzhou, China.

Wendy Locks is a graduate student in the Department of Oriental Languages at the University of California at Berkeley.

Denis C. Mair, who received his M.A. in Chinese Literature from Ohio State University, is a free-lance translator. His translation of Memories of a Mendicant Life appears in the journal Chinese Sociology and Anthropology.

Philip Robyn received his B.A. and M.A. from San Francisco State University; he has also done graduate work in Oriental Languages and computational linguistics at the University of California at Berkeley. He is a free-lance scientific and literary translator and a free-lance editor for the University of California Press. His interests include Chinese history, philosophy, religion, and literature; the history of science and religion; and computational and recreational linguistics.

Betty Ting received her B.A. degree in English Language and Literature from the University of Shanghai. Following graduate work in the United States, she returned to China, where she worked for China Reconstructs as a writer, reporter, translator, and editor for 24 years. She currently works as an editor, translator, and free-lance writer in Los Angeles.

Maurice H. Tseng [b. Peking, China, 1927] attended Nanking University, graduated from George Washington University, and did graduate studies at the University of California at Berkeley, where he specialized in Chinese classical literature. A free-lance interpreter and author of and contributor to four books on Chinese language and literature, he taught at Yale, Stanford, and the University of California at Berkeley, and is currently Professor of Foreign Languages and Literatures at San Francisco State University. Among his several community outreach activities, he is a founder and president of the Board of Directors of the newly established Chinese-American Bilingual School in San Francisco.

Judi Wong is a graduate student in the Chinese Program at San Francisco State University.

Ellen Yeung received her M.A. in Chinese from San Francisco State University, where she now works as an instructor. She is the co-translator of Hsiao Hung's The Field of Life and Death and the translator of Jun Qing's Dawn on the River (excerpt).

About
the
Editor

Howard Goldblatt is Associate Professor of Chinese at San Francisco State University. He is the author of Hsiao Hung (1976), co-translator of Chen Jo-hsi's The Execution of Mayor Yin (1978), and translator of Hsiao Hung's The Field of Life and Death (Ellen Yeung, co-translator) and Tales of Hulan River (1979), and Hwang Chun-ming's The Drowning of an Old Cat (1980). His current research involves the Northeastern group of writers, which includes Xiao Jun, who is represented in the present anthology. For the 1981-1982 academic year Professor Goldblatt is a Visiting Associate Professor of Chinese in the Oriental Languages Department of UCLA.